高中英语
语法语用研究
与实践

杨正仁　陶银烜 ◎ 主编

吉林教育出版社

图书在版编目（CIP）数据

高中英语语法语用研究与实践 / 杨正仁，陶银烜主编. — 长春：吉林教育出版社，2021.11

ISBN 978-7-5553-9306-1

Ⅰ.①高… Ⅱ.①杨…②陶… Ⅲ.①英语—语法—高中—教学参考资料 Ⅳ.①G634.413

中国版本图书馆CIP数据核字（2021）第215675号

高中英语语法语用研究与实践	杨正仁　陶银烜　主编
责任编辑　朱　欣	**装帧设计**　言之凿

出版　吉林教育出版社（长春市同志街1991号　　邮编　130021）

发行　吉林教育出版社

印刷　北京政采印刷服务有限公司

开本　787毫米×1092毫米　1/16　**印张**　16　**字数**　288千字

版次　2022年4月第1版　**印次**　2022年4月第1次印刷

书号　ISBN 978-7-5553-9306-1

定价　45.00元

编 委 会

随着全球化进程的不断加快，英语学习显得越来越重要。为了顺应世界教育改革发展潮流，教育部提出英语学科核心素养观，即"语言能力、文化品格、思维品质和学习能力"。其中，不管是开展语言知识和技能的教学还是育人层面的培养，其目的都是实现外语学习"工具性与人文性"的完美结合。而语法作为语言知识内容的重要组成部分，在学生英语核心素养培养中具有非常重要的作用。

　　语法是英语学习不可或缺的重要板块，也是学好英语这门学科的重要环节。然而我们从多年的英语教学中发现，学生始终认为语法是学习英语的难点，学生在英语语法学习方面或多或少存在一些问题与困惑。为了帮助学生启迪新思维、开辟新方法，在有限的时间内高效率地学懂语法、学好语法，从而使学生掌握语言规律，更好地进行听、说、读、看、写等实践活动，更好地培养学生在英语学科核心素养方面的能力，我们根据《普通高中英语课程标准（2017年版）》和《英语考试大纲》，结合自己的教学实际编写了此书。

　　我们在广泛调研和大量积累的基础上，注意该书的工具性、条理性、实用性和前瞻性，同时考虑语法的难度、运用和考试等方面的因素，编写时在顺序方面有所调整，没有编写语法中一些细枝末节的东西，更有利于学生在高考复习中参考学习。本书旨在帮助学生建构科学有效的思维方式，教会学生思考问题和解决问题的方法。本书语法详解部分对语法要点进行了详细透彻的阐述，以大量的语言素材（例句）为基础，语言接地气、实用、鲜活且富有时代感，为学生提供了良好的语用环境。讲练结合，每章设置从易到难的单句语法填空、单句改错、语法填空和短文改错等各种题型。习题汇集了历年高考真题以及学生容易出错的典型题，每道题逐一对应配置答案，可以用来随时检测，有效训练。目的是帮助学生通过这些语言材料及时掌握该章语法要点并加以运用，让语法真正成为为学生服务的工具。

　　时代在前进，社会在发展，教学改革也在不断推进，英语语法学习的思路和方法也会在实践中不断发展和创新。由于时间仓促、水平有限，编写中难免存在不足之处，希望大家批评指正，也希望大家提出宝贵的意见和建议，以便我们在今后的工作中做得更好。最后，衷心希望大家能突破语法难点，让语法服务于英语学习，达到真正运用语言的目的。

编　者

2020年4月

目录
CONTENTS

第一章　名　词

一、名词概述

表示人、事物、地点以及抽象概念的词叫作名词。名词通常分为专有名词和普通名词。专有名词的第一个字母必须大写，由两个以上普通名词构成的专有名词，其前面要加定冠词且每一个实词的第一个字母必须大写，如：China，California，Johnson，the People's Republic of China，the United Kingdom of Great Britain and Northern Ireland。普通名词分为可数名词和不可数名词，可数名词又分为个体名词（doctor，teacher，tree，book）和集体名词（family，people，police，cattle），表示人和物；不可数名词又分为物质名词（salt，sand，oil，glass）和抽象名词（performance，advice，information，fun），表示事物品质和感情。名词词义辨析、名词所有格以及名词作定语的用法是学习的重点。

二、名词的复数

（1）一般情况直接加-s，如：students，bikes，houses，dogs。

（2）以s，x，ch，sh结尾的名词加-es，如：buses，boxes，watches，bushes。但如果ch发/k/时，只加-s，如stomachs。

（3）以辅音字母加y结尾的名词，把y变为i，再加-es，如：factories，victories，families。

（4）以f，fe 结尾的名词，一般把f，fe 变为v，再加-es，如：thieves，shelves，wolves，wives，knives，loaves，halves，leaves，calves，selves，lives。可把这些常见名词编成顺口溜以便记忆：**小偷架下学狼叫，妻子拿刀切面包，半片叶子风吹掉，小牛自己把命逃。**

但有些以f, fe结尾的名词直接加-s, 如: cliffs, hoofs, chiefs, stiffs, gulfs, serfs, beliefs, proofs, handkerchiefs, roofs。编成顺口溜为: **老马悬崖失前蹄, 首领拄杖海湾区, 农奴相信有证据, 手绢飞到屋顶去。**

（5）以o结尾的名词一般加-s, 如: photos, radios, pianos, zoos。但下列名词常加-es, 如: zeroes, volcanoes, Negroes, heroes, tomatoes, potatoes。编成顺口溜为: **零点火山爆发时, 黑人英雄正吃土豆西红柿。**其中zero, volcano还可以直接加-s。

（6）合成名词如果有主体名词, -s加在主体名词后, 如: passers-by, new-comers, fathers-in-law, mothers-in-law, sons-in-law, sisters-in-law。合成名词如果没有主体名词, -s加在合成词词尾, 如: go-betweens（中介）, grown-ups（成人）, forget-me-nots（勿忘我）, touch-me-nots（含羞草）等。

（7）常见不规则变化的名词复数:

sheep—sheep 绵羊   deer—deer 鹿
fish—fish 鱼   means—means 手段
Chinese—Chinese 中国人   foot—feet 脚、英尺
man—men 男人   woman—women 女人
formula—formulae 公式   child—children 孩子
mouse—mice 老鼠   louse—lice 虱子
tooth—teeth 牙齿   goose—geese 鹅
bacterium—bacteria 细菌   crisis—crises 危机
thesis—theses 论文   analysis—analyses 分析
ox—oxen 公牛   medium—media 媒体
criterion—criteria 标准   phenomenon—phenomena 现象

（8）数字、字母等的复数形式:

in the 1930s=in the 1930's

3 w's 三个w

two but's and three if's 两个but三个if

three do's and three don't's 三要三不要

all of my 5's look like 8's 我所有的5看起来像8

（9）单复数意义不同的一些名词：

arm 胳膊—arms 武器　　　　　air 空气—airs 姿势、架子

brain 脑子—brains 智能　　　　compass 指南针—compasses 圆规

custom 风俗—customs 海关　　　day 日子—days 时代、时期

force 力量—forces 军队　　　　glass 玻璃—glasses 眼镜

green 绿色—greens 青菜　　　　iron 铁、熨斗—irons 手铐

line 线条，成行—lines 台词、对白　manner 方式—manners 礼貌

paper 纸—papers 文件、试卷　　snow 雪—snows 积雪

spirit 精神—spirits 酒精、情绪　sand 沙子—sands 沙滩

time 时间—times 时代、次数　　work 工作—works 作品

water 水—waters 水域　　　　wood 木头—woods 树林

（10）有些不可数名词也可以用作可数名词，但意思不同。例如：

beauty 美—a beauty 一个美人

character 性格—a character 一个汉字

success 成功—a success 一个成功的人、一件成功的事情

failure 失败—a failure 一个失败的人、一件失败的事情

knowledge 知识—a knowledge of something 精通、掌握……

relation 关系—a relation 亲戚

difficulty 困难—a difficulty 一件困难的事情

pleasure 乐趣—a pleasure 一件愉快的事情

experience 经验—an experience 一次经历

surprise 惊讶—a surprise 一件令人惊讶的事情、一个令人惊讶的人

三、不可数名词

下列不可数名词通常没有复数形式，可称为绝对不可数名词，如：
advice，news，information，fun，weather，equipment，furniture，luggage，baggage，jewellery等。例如：

What **fun** it is to have such a cold drink in such hot weather!

大热天喝这么冰冷的饮料是多么爽的事啊！

My teacher gave me a good piece of **advice** on how to write a composition.

我的老师就如何写作文给了我很好的建议。

Yesterday I bought a lot of **furniture** to furnish my new house.

昨天我买了很多件家具来装饰我的新房子。

四、名词所有格

（1）用于有生命的名词之后，如：the boy's bike，Tom's brother，the man's wallet。

（2）用于表示时间、距离、重量、价值、国家、城市等的名词之后，如：tomorrow's homework，an hour's walk，100-pound's weight，China's economy，California's treasure。

（3）复数名词所有格加在复数形式之后，如：the boys' bikes，the students' duty。

（4）表示两者共有时，所有格加在后一个名词后，如：Tom and Jim's room。

（5）表示两者分别拥有时，所有格加在每个名词后，如：Tom's and Jim's rooms。

（6）所有关系也可用of来表示，多用于无生命的名词和名词化了的词，也可用于有生命的名词。例如：

the legs of the chair 椅子腿

the color of the windows 窗户的颜色

the worry of the rich and the happiness of the poor 富人的忧愁和穷人的快乐

the dormitory of the first-year students 一年级学生的寝室

注意下列两组名词所有格的区别：

a picture of my father 我爸爸的一张照片（照片上拍的是我爸爸）

a picture of my father's 属于我爸爸的一张照片（照片上可以是任何人和东西）

a friend of my mother 我妈妈的一位朋友（强调和妈妈是朋友关系）

a friend of my mother's 我妈妈的一位朋友（强调是妈妈朋友中的一个）

五、名词的作用

名词在句中充当主语、宾语、表语、同位语、补语、状语及定语。例如：

The **dictionary** is very useful and I always keep it at hand.（主语）

这本字典很有用，我总是把它放在手边。

He borrowed some **money** from the **bank** on condition that he returned it within a year.（宾语）

他向银行借了一些钱，条件是一年内归还。

When she was a primary **student**, she used to be **monitor**.（表语）

当她是小学生的时候，她经常当班长。

Mr Wang, **president** of our school, often helps the man, a **farmer** in the rural area.（同位语）

我们的校长王先生经常帮助那个人——来自农村的一位农民。

They elected Mary **monitor** of our class and they often called her **sister**.（宾补）

他们选玛丽当我们班长并经常叫她姐姐。

I have told him **many times** to make the meetings short but today's meeting lasted 3 hours.（状语）

我告诉他好多次要开短会，但今天的会又持续了3个小时。

注意：名词作定语时多用单数形式，常表示材料、时间、用途、类别、功能、来源等。例如：

paper tiger 纸老虎
stone bridge 石桥
morning break 早间休息
coffee cup 咖啡杯
eye drops 眼药水
weather forecast 天气预报
feature film 故事片
press conference 记者招待会
power plant 发电厂

cotton goods 棉织品
afternoon tea 下午茶
evening news 晚间新闻
inquiry office 咨询处
time table 时间表
express train 快车
head nurse 护士长
news broadcast 新闻广播
shoe factory 鞋厂

Exercise One

（一）单句语法填空

1. Earth Day is an annual event to raise public＿＿＿＿＿（aware）about environmental protection.

2. I soon realized that my mom's greatest＿＿＿＿＿（strong）was taking care of those who cannot advocate for themselves and need trustworthy care providers.

3. There are more and more vendors' stands along the street filled with a great ＿＿＿＿＿（vary）of Spring Festival goods that catch the eye.

4. It was he who first stepped up private schools and received students from every walk of life without＿＿＿＿＿（consider）of their social status.

5. It's a skill that helps you find new perspectives to create new＿＿＿＿＿（possible）and solutions to different problems.

6. The response came after inquiries poured in over the last two days following news reports claiming Cambridge started accepting China's gaokao scores from new ＿＿＿＿＿（applicant）.

7. Few people I know seem to have much desire or time to cook. Making Chinese ＿＿＿＿＿（dish）is seen as especially troublesome.

8. This has not only encouraged plant ＿＿＿＿＿（grow）, but also helped in increasing the water table （地下水位）in the surrounding areas of the farm.

9. My search for the answer continued until one day a text message came from a student of ＿＿＿＿＿（I）.

10. For＿＿＿＿＿（hundred）of years people believed that tea could cure illnesses, and they used it as medicine.

（二）单句改错

1. The speaker tells us that the key to his success is honest.

2. When they are eating bamboo leaf, their funny behavior will make me laugh.

3. If we go on a trip frequently, we can broaden our horizon and gain knowledges we cannot get from books.

4. Exercise also takes up a lot of my spare time, though I do think exercise is

important to my healthy.

5. The CRH trains are spacious, comfortable and run at a top speed of 350 kilometers per hour. They are seldom delayed and can guarantee the safe of travelers.

6. Stress sometimes can push you to make full preparation for a test.

7. After supper, we would play card games of all sort in the sitting room.

8. First, with my teacher's help, I used the equipments from the school lab to test the quality of the river water.

9. Last night we went to the barber's, where I met a friend of my brother.

10. When I was little, Friday's night was our family game night.

（三）语法填空

阅读下面材料，在空白处填入适当的内容（1个单词）或括号内单词的正确形式。

The original Chinese opera *Marco Polo*, based on the story of the Venetian explorer___1___ traveled along the ancient Silk Road in the 13th century, will___2___（stage）in September in Italy.___3___（write）in Chinese and performed by Western and Chinese singers, the work is the first original Chinese opera produced by Guangzhou Opera House for the Silk Road International League of Theaters. The league serves as a platform for the performing arts and was set up to promote cultural___4___（change）between China and other countries.

The process of making this opera has been a major effort of___5___（communicate）. The Venetian explorer is seen as a symbol of friendship. The opera describes the romance between Marco and a young Chinese woman named Chuan Yun, as well as the rise and fall of the two___6___（dynasty）—Song and Yuan. It took a team of international artists about three years to put the opera together. The composer combined___7___（tradition）Chinese folk elements with Mongolian music and Western classical music.

Marco Polo is___8___symbol of connecting cultures. Besides the___9___（significant）of completely composing for a Chinese opera, the opera___10___（deliver）something more, that is, love and peace.

（四）短文改错

假定英语课上老师要求同桌之间交换修改作文，请你修改你同桌写的以下作文。文中共有10处语言错误，每句中最多有两处。每处错误仅涉及一个单词的增加、删除或修改。

增加：在缺词处加一个漏字符号（∧），并在其下面写出该加的词。

删除：把多余的词用斜线（\）划掉。

修改：在错的词下画一横线，并在该词下面写出修改后的词。

注意：1. 每处错误及其修改均仅限一词。

2. 只允许修改10处，多者（从第11处起）不计分。

（此段说明性文字在以后练习中不再重复。）

The busy school's life started again a month ago. The more exciting part of it came in September when my classmates and I attended the very Heritage Across Borders Program which took place at Zhejiang University. The Program mainly focused at how heritage is valued and preserved. As young activities in heritage protection, we felt honored to meet the world's leading group of researchers and professional in heritage studies. We were deeply impressed by their skillful. Besides, their anecdotes were extreme interesting. China is highlighting what is known as cultural confident nowadays. But we are pride of our efforts to preserve the local heritage.

第二章 代 词

一、代词概述

用来代替名词和句子的词叫作代词，它具有名词和形容词的作用。代词在句中主要充当主语、宾语、表语、定语、主语补足语或宾语补足语。作主语时用主格，作动词和介词的宾语时用宾格，作表语时也要用宾格。代词通常分为以下几类：

（1）人称代词（主格）：I, we, you, he, she, it, they。

（2）人称代词（宾格）：me, us, you, him, her, it, them。

（3）物主代词（形容词性）：my, our, your, his, her, its, their。

（4）物主代词（名词性）：mine, ours, yours, his, hers, its, theirs。

（5）反身代词：myself, ourselves, yourself, yourselves, himself, herself, itself, themselves。

（6）相互代词：each other, one another。

（7）指示代词：this, that, these, those, such, same（相同的那个人或事）。

（8）不定代词：all, each, every, both, either, neither, one, none, little, few, a little, a few, many, much, other, another, some, any, someone, something, somebody, anyone, anybody, anything, everyone, everybody, everything, nobody, nothing。

（9）疑问代词：who, whom, whose, what, which, whoever, whomever, whatever, whichever。

（10）连接代词：who, whom, whose, what, which, whoever,

whatever, whichever, that。

（11）关系代词：who, whom, whose, which, that, as。

二、代词用法疑难辨析

1. one, the one, ones, the ones, it, that, those

one 用来指前面提到的可数名词中的一个，等于"不定冠词+名词"；特指时用the one，等于"定冠词+名词"。

ones 泛指前面提到的复数名词，特指时用the ones，特指时往往有后置定语。

it特指前面提到的那个东西。

that特指前面提到的单数可数名词、不可数名词或者句子，可数名词后接"of..."定语时也用that。

those 用来特指或代替前面提到的复数名词或者指人，但一定不能用these代替。例如：

There are a great many English-Chinese dictionaries in that bookstore. I'm going to buy **one**.

那家书店有很多英汉词典，我打算买一本。

I don't like this green apple and please give me a red **one**.

我不喜欢这个绿色的苹果，请给我一个红色的。

The bicycle you bought yesterday is more expensive than **the one** that my father bought for me.

你昨天买的自行车比我爸爸给我买的贵。

I prefer red apples to yellow **ones**.

我喜欢红苹果而不是黄苹果。

The oranges you brought here are a great deal sweeter than **the ones** I bought yesterday.

你拿来的橘子比我昨天买的要甜得多。

There is no more than one such reference book in the bookstore and I'm going to buy **it** at once.

书店里仅有一本这样的参考书了，我打算立刻把它买回来。

—I was criticized by my math teacher yesterday.

我昨天被数学老师批评了。

—How was **that**?

那是怎么回事？

The weather in Beijing is much better than **that** in Tibet.

北京的天气比西藏好得多。

The mobile phone today is much more advanced than **that** of the past.

今天的手机比过去的先进得多。

Equipped with modern facilities，the libraries nowadays differ greatly from **those** of the past.

配备了现代化设施后，现在的图书馆和过去的图书馆有了巨大的差别。

2. none，no one（nobody），nothing

none 既可指人也可指物，用来回答how many，how much 的问题，后面还可接of us等短语。

no one（nobody）只能指人，用来回答who的问题，后面不能接of us等短语。

nothing只能指物，常用来回答what的问题，后面不能接of them等短语。

例如：

—How many tigers are there in the zoo？ —**None**.

这个动物园有多少只老虎？ —— 一只也没有。

—How much money do you have now？ —**None**.

你现在有多少钱？ —— 一点都没有。

—Who is still in the chemistry laboratory？ —**No one（Nobody）**.

谁还在化学实验室？ ——没人。

—What is in the bottle？ —**Nothing** except air.

瓶子里是什么？ ——除了空气之外，什么都没有。

None of the students in our school carries a mobile phone when they are at school.

上学期间，我们学校的学生中没有一位带手机的。

3. some, any, few, a few, little, a little, not a little, not a bit

some 常用于肯定句，但也可用于疑问句，表达诚意或者希望得到对方的肯定回答；any 多用于否定句、疑问句和条件句中，表示"一些"。

few，a few代替和修饰可数名词，few表示否定，a few表示肯定。

little，a little代替和修饰不可数名词，little表示否定，a little表示肯定；not a little = much or very，表示"很多"或"非常"，而not a bit = not at all，表示"一点也不"。例如：

If you have any interesting books, please give me **some** to read.

如果你有任何有趣的书的话，请给我几本读一读。

—Would you like **some** coffee?

你想喝咖啡吗？

—Yes. And would you please give me **some** without sugar?

是的。你能给我一些不加糖的吗？

—Are there **any** Internet-bars nearby?

附近有网吧吗？

—Yes, there are **a few**, but **few** students would like to go there.

是的，有几个，但几乎没有学生愿意去那儿。

—Would you like some sugar?

你想要糖吗？

—Yes, **a little. Little** is left in my box.

是的，要一点儿。我的盒子里几乎没有了。

Don't worry. There is **not a little** time left.

别担心，还剩下很多时间呢。

The movie was **not a little** interesting and many people queued to buy tickets.

这部电影非常有趣，因此很多人排队买票。

The lecture was **not a bit** attractive, so some people went out of the lecture hall one by one.

那个讲座一点都不吸引人，因此有些人一个接一个地离开了大厅。

4. another, other, the other, others, the others

another表示三者以上中的"另一个"，后接单数名词，但也可以说another

ten boys。

other后跟单数或者复数名词，表示"别的……"；the other 强调两者中的"另一个"，通常是one...the other...结构。

注意：ten other boys = ten more boys = another ten boys。

others 泛指"别人或别的东西"，后面不能再接名词，而the others则特指在一定范围内的"别人或者别的东西"，后面也不能接名词。例如：

I don't like the color of this jacket. Would you please show me **another**?

我不喜欢这件夹克的颜色。请你给我再拿一件好吗？

I'm afraid I will not go to the cinema with you. For one thing，I am busy with my homework；**for another**，my parents don't allow me to.

恐怕我不能和你一起去看电影，一则我忙于做作业，再则我爸妈不许我去。

There are more Native Americans living in California than in any **other** state today.

今天住在加利福尼亚州的美洲土著人比任何其他州都多。

No matter what **other** people say，I will do as I was told by my teacher.

无论别人说什么，我都会按照老师告诉我的去做。

She cannot get the first prize in writing competition. On one hand，there are some grammar mistakes in her composition；on **the other** hand，she doesn't employ genuine English expressions.

她在写作比赛中不能得一等奖。一方面，她的作文中有些许语法错误；另一方面，她没有用地道的英语表达。

He，like Lei Feng，is too ready to help **others**.（others = other people）

他像雷锋一样，太乐于助人了。

There are fifty students in our class. Forty of us are from the town we live in and **the others** are southerners.

我们班有五十名学生，四十名来自本市，其他的是南方人。

5. all，both

all表示三者以上的"全部"，后跟单数名词时表示"整个"，指所有的人时谓语动词用复数，指所有的事时谓语动词多用单数，含有all的句子中任何位置加not就是部分否定，它的完全否定用none表示。

both表示"二者都"，含有both的句子中任何位置加not也是部分否定，它的完全否定用neither表示。

all，both均位于实义动词之前，系动词、助动词、情态动词之后，也置于定冠词和限定词之前。例如：

All the windows of our classroom have been covered because of strong sunlight outside.

=The windows of our classroom have **all** been covered because of strong sunlight outside.

我们教室所有的窗户都因外面光线太强而被覆盖了。

All the people are here.

所有的人都在这里。

All that is to be done has been done.

所有该做的事都做好了。

Not all the young teachers in this school have opportunities to get further education.

=**All** the young teachers in this school **don't** have opportunities to get further education.

这所学校的年轻老师并不是都有机会去深造。（均为部分否定）

None of the young teachers in this school has / have opportunities to get further education.

这所学校的年轻教师都没有机会去深造。

Both my father and mother like playing table tennis.

我爸爸妈妈都喜欢打乒乓球。

My grandfather and grandmother **both** get up early in the morning and go exercising.

我爷爷奶奶早晨都早早起床去锻炼。

Both of my parents are **not** doctors. = **Not both** my parents are doctors.

我父母并非都是医生。（一个是医生，一个不是医生）

6. each, every, either, neither

each 强调个体，后加of us等短语；every强调全体，只作定语，后跟名词，但不能跟of us等短语； every two days，every other day，every second day中的 every不能被each代替。

either 表示两者中的"任何一个"，neither表示两者中"任何一个都不"，either...or...，neither...nor...用来连接两个平等成分，若连接两个主语时，谓语动词要就近一致。例如：

Each of the students has a mobile phone.

每个学生都有一部手机。（强调每个学生）

Every student has a mobile phone.

全体学生都有手机。（强调全体学生）

They come to work **every** two days / **every** other day / **every** second day.

他们每隔一天来上一次班。

There is coffee and beer in the kitchen and you can have **either**.

厨房内有咖啡和啤酒，你可以喝任何一种。

Neither of my parents is a doctor.

我爸爸妈妈都不是医生。

Neither of you has been chosen to take part in the final competition.

你们俩都没有被选上去参加决赛。

You should read English aloud **either** in or outside the classroom.

你既可以在教室内也可以在教室外大声地朗读英语。

Either you **or** I am mad.

要么你要么我疯了。

Are **either** you **or** I mad?

是你疯了还是我疯了？

They **neither** go to the cinema **nor** surf the Internet playing games while at school.

上学期间他们既不去看电影也不去上网玩游戏。

Neither the students in the class **nor** the head teacher was injured in the Yushu earthquake.

那个班的学生和班主任老师在玉树地震中都没有受伤。

7. whatever，whichever，whoever，whomever

whatever表示"无论什么"，既可以引导让步状语从句，等于no matter what，也可以引导名词性从句，等于anything that，还可以作疑问代词。与whichever相比，它一般没有范围限制。

whichever表示"无论哪个"，功能和whatever一样，但是有范围限制。

whoever表示"无论谁"，功能和whatever一样，引导名词性从句时等于anyone who；whomever也表示"无论谁"，但它是宾格形式。例如：

Whatever / No matter what you say, he will do as he likes.

无论你说什么，他都将做自己想做的事。

She will go to the library to search for whatever/anything that she could find about Mark Twain.

她将去图书馆找关于马克·吐温的任何能找到的东西。

Whichever team wins the final match will be chosen to participate in the national championship.

无论哪个队赢了决赛都将被选上去参加全国锦标赛。（范围就是所有参赛队）

Whichever / No matter which book you like on my bookshelf, you can take it home to read.

无论你喜欢我书架上的哪本书，你都可以带回家读。

Whichever university of China do you like to attend?

你到底喜欢上中国的哪所大学？

We will give those books to whoever badly needs them. (whoever = anyone who)

我们把那些书给非常需要的任何人。

Whoever / No matter who he or she is, I will do official business according to official principles.

无论他（她）是谁，我都会公事公办的。

Whoever has broken my glasses?

到底谁把我的眼镜打碎了？

You can invite whomever（whoever）you like to the party.

你可以邀请任何你喜欢的人参加晚会。

8. everyone，every one，nothing but，anything but，something like，something of

everyone指"每个人"，后面不能跟of us等短语；every one既可指"每个人"，也可指"每个东西"，但后面可接of us等短语。

nothing but表示"只是"，anything but表示"绝不是"，something like表示"有点像"，something of表示"有点"。例如：

Everyone in our class studies very hard and finishes homework on time.

我们班每个人都学习努力且按时完成作业。

Every one of us is in favor of the plan that we should finish five units every week.

我们中的每个人都支持每周完成五个单元的计划。

I searched **every one** of the libraries in the town but I didn't find the material I needed.

我找遍了城里的每一个图书馆，但是没找到我所需要的材料。

She is **nothing but** a nurse，but she is **something of** a woman professor.

她只是个护士，但她有点女教授的范儿。

He looks **something like** a porter，but he is **anything but** a lower-class worker.

他看起来有点像搬运工，但他绝不是一名底层工人。

Exercise Two

（一）单句语法填空

1. Nervously facing challenges, I know I will whisper to_____（I）the two simple words "Be yourself".

2. You can depend on_____that he will come to your help when needed.

3. Why do many of us find_____difficult or impossible to fall asleep in a bed other than our own?

4. *Letters Alive* took_____（it）idea from a UK program, *Letters Live*, released in 2013.

5. Nowadays, reference books have become a problem of great concern for _____the teachers and students.

6. In 1963 the UN set up the World Food Programme, one of_____purpose is to

relieve worldwide starvation.

7. It is all right to have a tiger in a cage, but to have_____in the driver's seat is another matter.

8. In many ways, the education system in the U.S. is not very different from _____ in the U.K.

9. At first she took my hands in_____ (she) and she listened patiently as I mentioned my worries.

10. It's a good place to spend the long hot summer. I love it from the bottom of_____ (me) heart.

（二）单句改错

1. Being the only child in the family, most teenagers like I grow up lonely, which does harm to our psychological health.

2. It's an either-or situation— we can buy a new car or we can go on holiday this year but we can't do either.

3. From then on, I started to play football with some another boys of my school after class.

4. While I agree with most of what you said, I don't agree with anything.

5. Many of the students are against the rule, arguing that the mobile has become a necessary part of their life. They also consider that a must for them to get relaxed from their busy studies.

6. Just then a bird was flying above our heads. My uncle immediately jumped up and shot the arrows at the bird. Neither of the arrows hit the target. Suddenly, the arrows were flying down like rain.

7. That is universally acknowledged that the poetry of the Tang Dynasty is one of the solid foundations of Chinese culture.

8. I read the announcement of the summer camp that you have posted it on the Internet and I am interested in it.

9. Johnson, please give the note to who is in the office.

10. The teacher said to Mary , "If you can't believe in you, nobody in this world may believe in you."

（三）语法填空

阅读下面材料，在空白处填入适当的内容（1个单词）或括号内单词的正确形式。

Texting while walking is something that most of us are guilty of. We can't help ___1___ （reply） to that message we just received. However, while ___2___ is fun to keep up with the latest news, we may actually be putting ___3___ （we） in danger. "I spotted a person in front of me walking very slowly and weaving and I thought, 'Is this person drunk?' But it turned out that the person was just texting." said Matthew Timmis.

___4___ （inspire） by this, Timmis and his team set out to seek the effects of phone use on ___5___ （passer-by）. A group of 21 volunteers were asked to walk around a certain street. The participants traveled the course a total of 12 times each, ___6___ writing or reading a message, making a call, or with no phone at all. ___7___ took the volunteers 118 percent longer to complete the course when using a phone. They also focused ___8___ the path 51 percent more when they weren't using a phone. Although there were no accidents, Timmis believes we should still be aware of ___9___ is going on around us. "You are not going to be able to respond to danger effectively, ___10___ increases the risk of injury." He added.

（四）短文改错

Many a child takes what their parents do for themselves for granted. They haven't realized the meaning of be grateful. But they always get angry with their parents because they don't get what they want. My friend once told me the news that a little girl went out of the house and refuse to return home as his parents did not give her enough pocket money. I was so shocking to hear it. I would never ask many from my parents because I knew it was not easy for him to make a living. And I always feel so thankful for what they have offered to me. If someone who gives me a hand when I am in need, I will remember him. If I have a chance, I will pay him back. In short, it is a grateful heart makes us become kind people and create a harmonious environment.

第三章　形容词

一、形容词概述及其作用

描述人和事物的性质、状态或特征的词叫作形容词。形容词在句中常作定语、表语、补语和状语。

1. 作定语

（1）大部分形容词可以单独作定语，但某些形容词作定语要和定冠词the连用，如the only，the same，the following，the very，the main等。例如：

Sometimes old people are easily fooled by a simple trick.

有时候老年人容易被简单的花招愚弄。

This is the very person that I have been looking for.

这正是我一直以来在找的那个人。

One hundred years ago we may have been in the same family.

一百年前我们也许是同一个家族的。

（2）形容词作定语时，大多数情况下放在名词之前，但下列情况下要后置：

第一，当修饰something，anything，everything，nothing，somebody，anybody，everybody，nobody，someone，anyone，everyone，no one等不定代词时。例如：

Is there anything difficult in the text that you cannot understand?

课文中有任何你不理解的难点吗？

If you are busy，I have to ask somebody else to help me with my mathematics.

如果你忙的话，我不得不请别人来帮我学数学。

第二，当"介词+名词""形容词+介词""形容词+不定式"或其他短语作定语时。例如：

The person **in charge** won't come to meet us until the meeting is over.

负责人直到会议结束才来接见我们。

He is a good student **worthy of praise** in class.

他是一名值得在全班表扬的好学生。

A question **so difficult** to answer may not appear in the coming examination.

如此难回答的一道题也许不会出现在即将到来的考试中。

There was a path over there, **narrow and muddy**.

那边有一条路，又窄又泥泞。

第三，表示长度（long）、宽度（wide）、高度（high）、深度（deep）、厚度（thick）、年龄（old）等的形容词与数量词连用时。例如：

Our office is in a building **twenty storeys high**.

我们办公室在一栋二十层高的大楼里。

When her mother died she was only a girl **five years old**.

她母亲去世时，她只是一个5岁的小女孩。

In the middle of the forest there is a hole **fifty meters deep**.

森林中间有一个五十米深的洞。

第四，当表语形容词afraid，awake，alone，asleep，ashamed，alike，alive，aware以及副词here，there等作定语时。例如：

People **alive** should continue the cause of those who have died for the country.

活着的人应该继续完成那些为国家而死去的人的事业。

The climate **here** is quite hot and humid, which is suitable for those plants.

这儿的气候相当炎热潮湿，这一点很适合那些植物。

（3）有些词作前置定语和后置定语意义不同，如：

The **present** youngsters have quite different ideas about life and work from previous ones.

现在的年轻人对生活和工作的观念和以前的年轻人不同。

The youngsters **present** are mainly post graduates from different universities.

在场的年轻人主要是来自不同大学的研究生。

The **absent** students can possibly miss some important things in class.

心不在焉的学生有可能错过课堂上的重点内容。

The students **absent** today shall be required to give reasons to the president themselves.

今天缺席的学生必须亲自向校长解释理由。

（4）多个形容词作定语的排列顺序。一般可以归纳为九个字来记忆："限描大、形龄颜、籍物类"+名词，其中"限"包括冠词、指示代词、物主代词、名词所有格、数词等，"描"指修饰性的形容词，"大"包括大小、长短、高低等的形容词，"形"包括方、圆、扁、平等的形容词，"龄"包括年龄、新旧、温度等的形容词，"颜"即颜色，"籍"即国籍、地区等，"物"即物质、材料，"类"包括类别、用途、目的等。例如：

I have **a lovely small new woolen** dog.

我有一只新的可爱的小羊毛狗。

One hundred strong young Chinese boys have been chosen to take part in the training.

一百名年轻强壮的中国男孩已经被选出来去参加培训。

2. 作表语

大部分形容词作表语时，主语可以是表示人的名词或代词，但有些形容词作表语时，不能用表示人的词作主语，如convenient, possible, probable, necessary等。例如：

Most students in our class are **outgoing** while some are quite **introverted**.

我们班大部分学生性格外向，而有一些相当内向。

Come and chat with me in my house whenever it is **convenient** to you.

无论什么时候方便你都可以来我房间聊天。

If it is very **necessary** for you to buy that car, I would like to lend you some money.

你如果非常有必要买那辆车的话，我会借钱给你的。

3. 作补语

形容词作宾补，位于宾语之后，说明宾语的状态、特征。例如：

The boss kept us **busy** working every day but didn't pay us extra money.

老板让我们每天忙着干活，但不给我们额外的钱。

She was made very **unhappy** by the loss of a large amount of money.

她因丢失一大笔钱而被弄得很不高兴。

After a day's hard work，he went home，**tired and hungry**.

一天的艰辛工作之后，他回到家里，又累又饿。

Robinson Crusoe hurried back home，**full of fear**.

鲁滨逊·克鲁索匆匆回到家里，心里充满恐惧。

He lay in bed，**awake and nervous**.

他躺在床上，醒着、忐忑着。

4. 作状语

形容词放置句首时，作状语，表示原因、状态等。例如：

Because tired and hungry，they went home for lunch.（表示原因）

因为又累又饿，他们回家吃午饭了。

Scared and cold，the Time Traveller starts back towards present.（表示状态）

又害怕又冷，时空旅人开始返回到现在。

二、复合形容词的作用及构成

复合形容词通常只作前置定语，复合形容词中的名词只用单数，常见构成如下：

1. 名词+形容词

Dolly the sheep is a **world-famous** clone，which lived only six and a half years.

多莉羊是一只世界著名的克隆羊，它只活了六岁半。

Our factory produces a lot of **duty-free** products，which will be sold to the countryside.

我们厂生产许多免税产品，它们将销往农村。

2. 名词+现在分词

There are many **English-speaking** countries in the world.

世界上有许多讲英语的国家。

We bought some **pest-killing** medicine in the crop hospital yesterday.

我们昨天在庄稼医院买了一些杀虫药。

3. 名词+过去分词

Is this a **man-made** cloning or natural one?

这是人工克隆还是自然克隆?

The **state-owned** company is difficult to enter，because they have high standards.

这家国有公司不好进，因为标准很高。

4. 数词+名词

She has a **ten-speed** bicycle，which was sent by her boyfriend as a birthday gift.

她有一辆十速自行车，那是男朋友送给她的生日礼物。

A lot of old people have entered for the **10,000-metre** race to be held next month.

许多老年人已经报名参加下个月将要举行的一万米赛跑。

5. 数词+名词+形容词

A **four-year-old** boy fell into a **two-meter-deep** hole，but fortunately he was not hurt.

一名四岁的男孩掉进一个两米深的洞里，但幸运的是他没受伤。

6. 数词+名词+ed

A **one-eyed** woman comfortably sat in a **six-legged** armchair reading.

一位独眼女子舒适地坐在一把六条腿的躺椅上阅读。

7. 形容词+名词

By coincidence our **mid-term** examination falls on **Mid-autumn** Festival.

我们的期中考试碰巧在中秋节那天。

8. 形容词+名词+ed

Our teacher is a **warm-hearted** lady，who gave us a lecture on **cold-blooded** animals yesterday.

我们老师是个热心肠的人，她昨天给我们做了一个关于冷血动物的报告。

9. 形容词+现在分词

The **good-looking** young man is an **easy-going** guy to deal with.

这位相貌好看的年轻人是一个容易相处的人。

10. 形容词+过去分词

Some **new-laid** eggs were found in a **new-built** henroost.

（人们）在一个新造的鸡窝中发现了一些新下的鸡蛋。

11. 副词+现在分词

What a **hard-working** teacher does usually has an **ever-lasting** effect.

一位辛勤的老师所做的工作通常会有久远的影响。

12. 副词+过去分词

A **well-educated** university graduate will be sent to work in a **newly-built** town.

一位受过良好教育的大学毕业生将被派到一个新建的镇上去工作。

三、形容词和副词的比较等级及其用法、同义形容词用法辨析

1. 形容词和副词比较级和最高级的构成

（1）单音节词的形容词和副词一般在词尾加-er，-est，如：thick—thicker，thickest。

（2）以字母e结尾的形容词和副词只加-r，-st，如：large—larger，largest。

（3）以重读闭音节结尾，末尾只有一个辅音字母，先双写辅音字母，再加-er，-est，如：thin—thinner，thinnest；red—redder，reddest；fat—fatter，fattest；hot—hotter，hottest。

（4）以辅音字母加y结尾的形容词和副词，变y为i，再加-er，-est，如：happy—happier，happiest；early—earlier，earliest；dirty—dirtier，dirtiest。

（5）部分双音节词和多音节词在前面加上more，most构成比较级和最高级，如：interesting—more interesting，most interesting；important—more important，most important。

（6）有些双音节词既可以加-er，-est，也可以加more，most，如：common，handsome，polite，tired，quiet，bitter，stupid，pleasant，cruel等。

（7）常见不规则变化的形容词和副词有：good—better，best；well—better，best；bad—worse，worst；badly—worse，worst；ill—worse，worst；many—more，most；much—more，most；far—farther / further，farthest / furthest；old—older / elder，oldest / eldest。

2. 形容词和副词比较等级的用法

（1）形容词和副词比较级和最高级的常见句型：

She is **as hard-working as** her sister but she is **not so**（**as**）**outstanding as** her sister.

她和姐姐一样勤奋但不及姐姐出众。（否定句中才能用so...as）

The population of China is much **larger than** that of Japan.

中国的人口比日本多得多。

The population of China is much **larger than** that of any country in Europe.

中国的人口比欧洲任何一个国家都多。（中国不属于欧洲）

The population of China is much **larger than** that of any **other** country in Asia.

中国的人口比亚洲其他任何一个国家都多。（中国属于亚洲，所以加other）

I love you **more than** him.

我比他更喜欢你。或：我喜欢你胜过喜欢他。

I love you **more than** he.

我比他更喜欢你。

The more money a person has，**the more greedy** he / she will become.

一个人越有钱就变得越贪婪。

I am sure our country is getting **more and more beautiful and powerful**.

我相信我们的国家会变得越来越美丽和强大。

There are two boys standing under the tree，**the taller** of whom is my son.

树下站了两个男孩，个头高的那个是我儿子。

The questions in the examination paper were easy，you could have done **better**.

试卷上的问题简单，你完全可以做得更好。

How wonderful the movie is! I have never seen **a more exciting** one before.

这部电影太好了！我以前从来没看过一部比这更令人兴奋的电影。

John is **the tallest** among the boys in his class.（形容词最高级须与定冠词连用）

约翰是班上男孩子中个头最高的。

John jumps（the）**highest** among the boys in his class.（副词最高级前可以不用定冠词）

约翰是班上男孩子中跳得最高的。

The Yellow River is **the second largest** river in China.

黄河是中国第二大河流。

（2）形容词和副词比较级常用修饰语：

much，far，even，still，rather，a lot，a great deal，by far，a little，a bit，a little bit，slightly，any，no，twice等，但一定不能用比较级修饰比较级，也不能用very，quite修饰比较级。例如：

—Are you feeling **any better** now?

你现在觉得好点了吗？

—Yes，**slightly better** than yesterday.

是的，比昨天好了一点。

He runs **a great deal faster** than all the other boys in his school.

他比他们学校其他男孩子跑得快得多。

（3）表达倍数的常见句型：

The meeting-room is **four times larger than** an ordinary classroom.

这间会议室比普通教室大四倍。

We eat **a little more than twice as many vegetables now as** we did ten years ago.

我们现在吃的蔬菜是十年前的两倍多一点。

Our playground is **twice the size of** yours.（常用名词length，width，depth，weight，height...）

我们的操场是你们的两倍大。

The area of the ocean is **about two and a half times as large as** the land.

海洋的面积大约是陆地面积的两倍半。

The production of cars now is **five times what it was ten years ago.**

现在汽车的产量是十年前的五倍。

（4）含有比较级的短语用法辨析：

no more = not any more 不再，no longer = not any longer 不再。

more than 超过，不仅仅，非常，与其……不如……。

no more than 仅仅，和……一样不，not more than 不超过，前者不及后者。

no less than 多达，not less than 至少，no less...than 和……一样。例如：

No more money from my parents will come into my account. （表数量 "不再" 多）

不再有来自父母的钱打入我的账户。

There is **no longer** duration for us to have a holiday. （表时段 "不再" 长）

不再有休假的时间了。

He will **not** come here to see me **any more**.（表动作 "不再" 重复）

他不会再来这儿看我了。

He will **not** stay here **any longer**.（表动作 "不再" 延续）

他将不再待在这里了。

There are **more than** four thousand students in our school.

我们学校有四千多名学生。

He is **more than** a doctor. Besides，he is a member of WHO.

他不仅仅是名医生，他还是世界卫生组织的一名成员。

The girl is **more than** pretty，so all the boys like her.

这个女孩非常漂亮，因此所有的男孩都喜欢她。

If you want to know how much I love you，I tell you I love you **more than** I can say.

如果你问我到底有多么爱你，我会告诉你：爱你在心口难开。

The blind man said the elephant was **more like** a snake **than** anything else.

那位盲人说，这头大象与其说像别的任何东西，倒不如说它像条蛇。

There is **no more than** five dollars left in my wallet.

我的钱包里只剩下五美元了。

She jumps **no higher than** her sister in Class Two.

她和她在二班的姐姐一样跳得不高。

There are **not more than** thirty students in each class，which is suitable for teaching a language.

每个班不超过三十名学生，这样适合教语言。

The film is **not more interesting than** the one I saw the other day.

这部电影不及我前几天看过的那部有趣。

There are **no less than** seventy students in each class in our school.

我们学校每个班多达七十名学生。

Erik can speak **not less than** six languages.

艾瑞克至少会讲六种语言。

The boy is **no less hard-working than** his elder sister.

这个男孩和他姐姐一样勤奋。

3. 最常见同义形容词用法辨析

（1）alone & lonely：

alone既可以作副词也可以作形容词，作形容词时只作表语和后置定语，同时也表示客观上"单独的，独自一人"，而lonely只用作形容词，代替alone作前置定语，同时表示主观上"孤独，寂寞"。例如：

Though he was **alone** on a **lonely** island, he didn't feel **lonely** at all.

尽管他独自一人在那个孤岛上，但他一点都不觉得寂寞。

（2）alive, living, live & lively：

alive作表语或后置定语，不能作前置定语；living既可作表语也可作定语，并且可代替alive作前置定语；live既可作形容词也可作副词，作形容词时多修饰动物，表示"活的"，修饰人时表示"精力充沛的、生龙活虎的"，也表示"现场直播的"；lively是形容词，表示"生动的、活泼的"。例如：

People **alive** should do what they can to help those whose families were destroyed in the earthquake.

活着的人应该竭尽全力帮助那些在地震中失去家的人。

The disaster brought great damage to those **living** things.

那场灾难给那些生物带来了巨大的损失。

The **live** old man caught a **live** bird and set free.

那位精力充沛的老人抓住了一只活鸟，然后把它放了。

The **lively** young teacher gave us a **lively** description about his life as a new teacher.

那位活泼的年轻老师给我们生动地描述了他作为一名新教师的生活经历。

（3）normal, common, ordinary, usual, general & typical：

normal表示"正常的，标准的，师范的"；common表示"普遍的、司空见惯的"；ordinary表示"普通的"，相对于special；usual表示"通常的、寻常的"；general表示"大体的、总体的"；typical表示"典型的"。例如：

A person with **normal** intelligence can go to a **normal** school.

一个有正常智力的人就可以上正规的学校。

Tom and Tim are very **common** names in English like "Long and Jun" in Chinese.

汤姆和蒂姆就像汉语中"龙"和"军"一样，是非常普遍的英文名字。

We **ordinary** people make up the majority of the whole population.

我们普通人（老百姓）占了总人口的大多数。

He got up earlier this morning than **usual**, because he was afraid his **usual** seat would be occupied by someone else.

他今天早晨起得比平常早，因为他担心他往常的座位被别人占了。

Read quickly through the text and get the **general** idea of it, please.

请快速浏览课文并找出课文大意。

It's **typical** of him to be late for meetings, so don't be angry.

开会迟到是他一贯的行为作风，因此你也不要生气。

（4）likely, possible & probable：

这三个词都表示"可能"，但likely的主语可以是人和物，也可以是形式主语it，而possible，probable多用在it作形式主语的句子中，probable比possible可能性更大一些。例如：

She is **likely** to come to the meeting this afternoon.

今天下午她有可能来开会。

It is **likely** to rain soon.（it指天气，故不能用其他两个词）

天有可能马上下雨。

It is **possible** / **probable** / **likely** for him to pass the driving test, because he practiced a lot.

他有可能通过驾驶测试，因为他练得多。

It is **possible** but not **probable** that she will marry a middle-aged man.

她有可能嫁给一个中年男子，但可能性不大。

4. 以-ly结尾的形容词

有些形容词以-ly结尾，看似副词，实际上是形容词，如：friendly，fatherly，motherly，comradely，lovely，lively，lonely，likely，deadly，silly，orderly，timely等。例如：

The **fatherly** teacher is very **friendly** to us and often gives us some **timely** advice.

这位父亲般的老师对我们很友好，并且经常给我们一些及时的建议。

Exercise Three

（一）单句语法填空

1. Teaching young children is a＿＿＿＿＿（challenge）and rewarding job.

2. It can be seen as a unique application of wireless technology, highlighting the high-quality products and＿＿＿＿＿（advance）technology provided by China's communication section.

3. This is a key step for BDS（中国北斗卫星导航系统）developing from a Chinese experimental system to a regional and＿＿＿＿＿（globe）navigation system.

4. Chinese products are＿＿＿＿＿（impress）and competitive and can go forward to keep pace with foreign brands.

5. Nowadays, not only does China have the＿＿＿＿＿（fast）growing modern cities in the world, but it has diverse landscapes.

6. The city government should release more detailed regulations about minsu（民宿）in urban and rural areas of Beijing no＿＿＿＿＿（late）than August 2, 2019.

7. To make things＿＿＿＿＿（bad）, my mother was discovered to have caught a serious disease.

8. The world's＿＿＿＿＿（powerful）computer is located in China while the fastest US computer Titan is ranked fifth.

9. In the vineyard, thanks to the hot and dry climate that results from being surrounded by desert, huge quantities of large and＿＿＿＿＿（juice）grapes with very thin skin are produced.

10. The stamps feature seven＿＿＿＿＿（forget）characters from Jin Yong's well-known novels.

（二）单句改错

1. A few minutes later, the instructor asked me to stop the car. It was a relief and I came to a suddenly stop just in the middle of the road.

2. Aside from emailing, she thinks that it feels greatly to talk to her grandchildren

on WeChat.

3. At that time, I was too shy to make new friends so I was very alone for a few weeks.

4. When I started college, I moved to other city, away from my family and old friends.

5. I was not an experiencing hiker and those endless steps made me want to return to the safe and comfortable ground.

6. Others students sang and danced happily.

7. We carried two backpacks, which turned out to be pretty heavier for the hike.

8. The flowers that I bought were Mom's favoritest.

9. I think that participating in after-school activities is very good for students. Therefore, every student should take part in at most one after-school activity.

10. As the saying goes, "The process is much beautiful than the outcome."

（三）语法填空

阅读下面材料，在空白处填入适当的内容（1个单词）或括号内单词的正确形式。

Jin Yong was a Chinese wuxia novelist, ____1____ cofounded the Hong Kong daily newspaper *Ming Bao* in 1959 and served as the first editor-in-chief. He was one of ____2____ （famous） writers in China.

His wuxia has a widespread following in Chinese communities worldwide. His 15 works ____3____ （produce） between 1955 and 1972 earned him a reputation as one of the greatest and most popular wuxia writers ever. Over 100 million ____4____ （copy） of his works have been sold worldwide. According to *The Oxford Guide to Contemporary World Literature*, Jin Yong's novels are ____5____ （high） evaluated and are able to appeal to both highbrow and lowbrow tastes. His works have the ____6____ （usual） ability to go beyond geographical and ideological barriers separating Chinese communities of the world, achieving ____7____ （great） success than any other contemporary writer.

His works ____8____ （translate） into many languages so far. There are many fans outside of Chinese-speaking areas, as a result of the ____9____ （number） adaptations of his works into films, television series, comics and video games.

Jin Yong is named along with Gu Long and Liang Yusheng as the "Three Legs of the Tripod of Wuxia" and the asteroid（小行星）10930 Jinyong（1988 CR2）is named___10___him.

（四）短文改错

As a middle school student of Senior Three, I do sports one or two hours a day, such as doing morning exercises, play basketball, long-distance running or so on. I think it is very helpfully for me. Take exercise makes me even more healthier so that I won't become ill very often. What's more, I also get myself relaxing in different kinds of sports. Only in this way I do a better job in my study with high spirits. By doing physics exercise, I'm becoming stronger and more confident than before. I do think it is unnecessary for us to do it every day because people's health is important in modern life.

第四章　副　词

一、副词概述及其作用

在句中表示行为或状态特征的词叫作副词，通常用来修饰动词、形容词、介词短语、非谓语动词、整个句子及其他副词，表示时间、地点、程度以及方式等。在句中常作状语、定语、表语以及补语。副词词义辨析及比较等级的用法是学习的重点。

1. 作状语

副词作状语时，经常修饰动词、形容词、介词短语、整个句子和其他副词。例如：

We were **warmly** welcomed by the local people when we visited the village.

我们在参观那个村子时受到当地人的热烈欢迎。

The questions in the exam paper are **extremely** difficult.

试卷上的题目非常难。

He has fallen **far** behind others in studies because of his illness.

由于生病，他在学习方面已经远远落在别人后面。

That is **exactly** what she told me when we met last time.

那正是上次见面时她告诉我的事。

Hopefully, all the students will be employed after they graduate from the university.

所有的学生从这所大学毕业以后都有望被录用。

He ran **fast** enough when he was in the 10, 000-metre race this morning.

他今天早晨在万米赛跑中跑得足够快。

2. 作定语

表示时间和地点的副词通常可用作后置定语，如：here，there，down，downstairs，upstairs，now，nowadays，then，today，tomorrow等。例如：

The girl **downstairs** is waiting for you，so please be quick!

楼下那个女孩在等你，因此，你快点啊！

The climate **there** is hot and wet in summer and cold and dry in winter.

那儿的气候夏天又热又湿，冬天又冷又干。

3. 作表语

副词作表语时多指主语的方位、方向等。例如：

Wherever you go，whatever you do，I'll be **right here** waiting for you.

无论你去哪里，无论你做什么，我都在这儿等你。

The sitting-room is **downstairs** but all the bedrooms are **upstairs**.

客厅在楼下，而所有的卧室都在楼上。

4. 作补语

副词常用作宾语补足语、主语补足语以及用于with复合结构中。例如：

I happened to see her **together** with you when I went shopping yesterday.

昨天我去购物时看见你和她在一起。

The little boy was last seen **upstairs** in his bedroom.

有人最后看见这个小男孩在楼上自己的卧室。

With so many people **around**，I couldn't concentrate on my work.

周围有那么多人，我无法集中注意力于工作。

二、副词的位置

副词作状语时，位置比较灵活，根据需要可以放置在句首、句中或者句末。修饰介词、形容词和副词时放在被修饰的词之前；修饰全句时可以放在句首，也可以放在句末；修饰动词时，常常放在行为动词之前，系动词、助动词和情态动词之后；多个副词作状语时的顺序通常是：地点、状态、次数、时间等；enough修饰形容词或副词时要后置。例如：

Just in the middle of the lake there is an island，on which there are some trees.

就在那个湖中央有一个岛屿，岛屿上面长着一些树。

Unfortunately, we didn't take enough food when we were stuck in traffic last month.

不幸的是，上个月我们遇到塞车时，没有带足够的食物。

She didn't tell me anything about their quarrel, **actually**.

实际上，她没告诉我任何关于他们吵架的事。

I **usually** do my homework in the evening.

我通常在晚上做作业。

She is **always** a lively and optimistic girl, as anyone knows.

正如大家所知道的那样，她一直是一个活泼乐观的女孩。

He has **already** finished writing the composition.

他已经写完了作文。

He can **also** speak French because it was his second foreign language at university.

他也会讲法语，因为法语是他上大学时的第二外语。

They arrived **here safely** for the first time **yesterday**.

他们昨天第一次安全到达这里。

Believe it or not, our classroom is big **enough** to seat 150 students.

信不信由你，我们教室大得足够可以容纳一百五十名学生。

She behaved **strangely enough** at the party yesterday evening.

她在昨晚的晚会上表现得够怪的。

三、最常见副词用法辨析

1. high & highly, deep & deeply, wide & widely, close & closely

不带-ly的词既可以用作形容词，也可以用作副词，这里主要谈它们作副词时的区别。

high表示具体的"高地"，而highly则表示抽象的"高度地"。

deep表示具体的"深地"，而deeply则表示抽象的"深深地"。

wide表示具体的"宽地、完全地"，经常修饰形容词open，awake等，而widely则表示抽象意义的"广泛地"。

close表示具体的"靠近、挨近"，而closely则表示抽象的"紧密地、仔细地"。例如：

The trainer asked the trainees to jump as **high** as possible.（高度具体，可测量）

训练者让被训练者尽可能往高跳。

His personal talent performance was **highly** thought of by all the judges.（高度抽象，不可测量）

他的个人才能展示得到所有评委的高度评价。

He didn't realize the potential danger and walked **deep** into the forest.（深度具体，可测量）

他没有意识到潜在的危险而走向森林深处。

All the people present were **deeply** moved by what the speaker said at the meeting.（深度抽象，不可测量）

所有在场的人都被会议发言人的话深深地打动。

He was **wide** awake and his eyes were **wide** open.（完全地，较具体）

他一点睡意都没有并且眼睛睁得很大。

As we know, English is becoming more and more **widely** used in many fields.（广泛地，不易测量）

据我们所知，英语在很多领域越来越广泛地被使用。

You better come over and stand **close** to me and I will protect you from any danger.（具体）

你最好过来站的离我近点，我会保护你不受任何危险侵害。

We must **closely** follow the Communist Party of China and serve the people well.（抽象）

我们必须紧密跟随中国共产党并且好好为人民服务。

2. direct & directly，free & freely，just & justly，sharp & sharply

不带-ly的词既可以用作形容词，也可以用作副词，这里主要谈它们作副词时的区别。

direct意为"直线地、不绕圈子地"，directly意为"立刻地、不耽误地"。

free意为"自由地、免费地"，freely意为"随便地、自如地"。

just意为"正好"，justly意为"公正地"。

sharp意为"急剧地、整整地"，sharply意为"严厉地"。例如：

The plane flew **direct** to Shanghai this morning.

这架飞机今天上午直飞上海。

Hearing the news, we drove **directly** to the accident spot.

听到消息以后，我们毫不耽误地开车到了事故现场。

My car is often repaired **free** in the garage.

我的车子经常在那家修理厂免费维修。

After learning English for five years, he can now express himself **freely**.

学了五年英语之后，他现在可以自如地表达自己。

He had **just** finished his homework when the lights went out.

他刚做完作业，灯就熄灭了。

His efforts were **justly** rewarded with a large amount of money.

这一大笔钱是对他努力的公正奖赏。

It is twelve o'clock **sharp** now and let's begin our lesson.

现在十二点整，让我们上课吧。

Demand for mobile phones is rising **sharply**.

人们对手机的需求急剧上升。

3. hard & hardly, fair & fairly, late & lately, most & mostly

不带-ly的词既可以用作形容词，也可以用作副词，这里主要谈它们作副词时的区别。

hard意为"努力地、凶猛地"，而hardly则意为"简直不"。

fair和fairly均可表示"公平地"，fair有"正好"之意，而fairly还可以表示"相当地、还算"等。

late意为"晚"，而lately = recently，意为"最近"。

most意为"非常"，而mostly = mainly，意为"主要地、大部分地"。例如：

He was working **hard** at his lessons in the classroom while it was raining **hard** outside.

外面下着大雨，他在教室里努力学习功课。

He could **hardly** answer the teacher's question at the moment in the class.

那会儿在课堂上，他简直不能回答老师的问题。

He is in charge of playing **fair** in the game.

他负责比赛公平进行。

The ball hit him **fair** on the head.

那个球正好打在他的头上。

All of them were **fairly** treated in the competition but only two of them did **fairly** well.

他们所有人在比赛中被公平对待，但只有两个人表现得还算不错。

She came back home **late** last night because of the heavy rain.

由于大雨，她昨晚回家晚了。

The teacher asked me whether I had heard from my sister **lately**.

老师问我最近有没有收到我姐姐的来信。

The film is a **most** interesting and instructive one and I want to see it again.

这部电影非常有趣味和教育意义，我还想看一次。

Our class is **mostly** made up of girls from different big cities.

我们班主要由来自不同大城市的女孩子组成。

4. too much & much too；too，also，either & as well

too much 和 much too 主要按照第二个词的用法而定，much修饰不可数名词，所以too much也修饰不可数名词，too修饰形容词和副词，所以much too也修饰形容词和副词。

too一般放在句末，用逗号隔开，also多用于句中或句首及not only...but also中，as well用于句末，不用逗号隔开，either用于否定句句末，用逗号隔开。例如：

There is **too much** homework for us middle school students every day.

我们中学生每天有太多的作业。

This kind of question is **much too** difficult for some students to answer.

这种问题对一些学生来讲太难回答。

If you go to the cinema instead of watching TV，I will go，**too**.

如果你去看电影而不看电视，我也去看电影。

She can **not only** speak English **but also** sing English songs.

她不仅会讲英语，还会唱英文歌曲。

He is not just good at learning foreign languages but he does well in science **as well**.

他不仅擅长学外语而且在科学方面也做得很好。

She doesn't like doing housework and her husband doesn't like it, **either**.

她不喜欢做家务活，她丈夫也不喜欢。

5. very，quite，rather&fairly

very意为"非常"，语气最强，修饰形容词和副词，但不能修饰比较级或动词，经常构成very much来修饰动词。

quite意为"相当地"，可以修饰形容词、副词和动词，也可以修饰possible，right，wrong，perfect等极端意义的形容词，但不能修饰比较级。

rather可以修饰形容词、副词以及比较级和too引起的短语，意为"稍微有点"。

fairly意为"相当地、公平地"，多用来修饰褒义的形容词和副词，不能修饰比较级。例如：

He is **very** clever and he likes to learn science **very much**.

他非常聪明并且非常喜欢学习科学。

I didn't **quite** follow you as what you said was **quite** a complicated problem.

因为你所讲的是个相当复杂的问题，所以我完全跟不上你。

It is **quite** possible for us to achieve our goals because we have made great efforts.

我们相当有可能实现目标，因为我们付出了极大的努力。

It is **rather** easier for us to finish the homework with the teachers' help than without it.

有老师的帮助比没有老师的帮助对我们来说完成作业容易得多。

It was **rather too** difficult for them to pass the driving test.

对他们来说，通过驾照考试稍微有点难。

The girl is **fairly** clever and she can answer the question correctly.

这女孩相当聪明，她能正确回答这个问题。

6. almost & nearly

almost可以和never，nobody，no one，nothing，no，none，too，more than搭配使用。

nearly前可用not修饰，意为"一点儿也不，相差甚远"，两者都可以修饰表极端意义的形容词。例如：

Almost nothing about the accident was mentioned at the meeting.

关于这个事故，会上几乎什么都没提到。

Almost no one came to the smoking area to smoke.

几乎没有人来吸烟区吸烟。

I was **not nearly** ready to speak，but I was asked to.

我一点都没准备，但被要求发言。

It is an **almost**（**a nearly**）perfect plan that has ever been made.

这是曾经做出的几乎完美的计划。

四、使用副词的注意事项

1. 副词最高级前可以不用the，其他用法同形容词。例如：

He runs（**the**）**fastest** in his school.

他是他的学校跑得最快的。

2. 动词和副词搭配构成短语时，代词作宾语要放在中间。例如：

He tried his best to stop smoking but it was difficult for him to **give it up**.

他竭尽全力戒烟，但是对他来说很难做到。

3. enough修饰形容词和其他副词时要后置，且构成cannot...enough = cannot too...，意为"……都不为过"。例如：

The hall is **big enough** to seat one thousand people.

这个大厅大得可以容纳一千人。

You **can never be careful enough** while driving the car.

=You **can never be too careful** while driving the car.

当你开车时怎么小心都不为过。

Exercise Four

（一）单句语法填空

1. Look _____（attentive）and you'll see that boat built with porcelain（瓷器）looks like a takeout box.

2. With its good quality and competitive price, the Shaxian Delicacies brings in over 10 billion *yuan* _____ （annual）.

3. The annual Ice and Snow Sculpture Festival is Harbin's main tourist highlight. It is the world's biggest winter festival. The _____ （bitter） cold winter is just right for the festival.

4. Most _____ （important）, if the environment continues to be polluted, various specious（似是而非）things will be put into danger.

5. A singer, for example, wore a shiny and _____ （heavy） decorated yellow gown（女礼服）to the gala to match the gala's theme "China: Through the Looking Glass".

6. In fact, the number of students who have decided not to start their careers within six months has been increasing _____ （steady） since 2011.

7. In northeast China, especially in summer, as the sky darkness, many people go to the night market to eat, drink and chat with family and friends _____ （relax）.

8. She _____ （far） explained that although this woman was old and bedridden（卧床不起的）, she was still a lady, and the old deserved to be treated with respect.

9. Recent studies show that we are far more productive at work if we take short breaks _____ （regular）.

10. It is _____ （certain） fun but the lifestyle is a little unreal.

（二）单句改错

1. Interesting, she had a special love of farm life at that time.

2. To begin with, WeChat is a relative cheap way of communication nowadays.

3. Only in this way can they keep pace with the rapid developing international world.

4. Personally, I feel strong that exercising does us lots of good. It can build up our strength and improve our physical state.

5. Then I couldn't wait to have a try. I admitted I was deep attracted by the Chinese calligraphy.

6. It was 10 o'clock when he returned back home, still quite frightened of what happened in the street.

7. I'm little of course, but terrible quick and brave.

8. The qualities of health care vary great in some different areas.

9. The number of students in this school has reduced down to 500 this year.

10. General speaking, there are many kinds of tea in China, including green tea, black tea and so on.

（三）语法填空

阅读下面材料，在空白处填入适当的内容（1个单词）或括号内单词的正确形式。

World Sleep Day falls ___1___ March 21.This year's theme concerns sleep and women.

More women suffer from insomnia（失眠） than men, but only 4 percent of them go to a doctor to get help. A newspaper reported ___2___（recent）. A study by an international organization in the paper said that women ___3___（age） 30 to 60 sleep six hours and 41 minutes a day on ___4___（average）.

Young people have also been shown to suffer from a lack of sleep. Statistics from a Chinese medical research center show that in cities like Beijing and Shanghai, 40 percent of young people suffer from insomnia, and 80 percent suffer from great tiredness due to poor quality sleep.

Experts blame heavy ___5___（press） and competition at work for poor ___6___（sleep） habits. The long-term effects can be unhappiness, anxiety and depression, ___7___ can in turn lead to chronic illnesses（慢性病）, ___8___（especial） in women.

There are, however, a couple of tricks for ___9___（get） a good sleep, such as maintaining an optimistic attitude, keeping a regular, ___10___（day） routine, or finding time for sports. Also, you can develop healthy habits, such as keeping the bedroom clean and avoiding tea, coffee, or wine before sleeping.

（四）短文改错

Last week, I read an article about whether it is appropriately to lend a hand if we see animals in the danger. This question was raised after the rescue of a group of penguins from an icy hole in Antarctica. A film crew was alarmed when seen that the penguins had fallen into the hole and trapped. They dig a road so that the penguins could save them. But every coin has two sides. Some people were happy to watch the animals being rescued safe. However, others thought which they did disobeyed the rule of nature. Personal, I think we should help animals, because animals and humans need each other. They are our friends and of great important.

第五章　冠词和数词

一、冠词

用来限制名词，表示"一个"或者"这个、那个"的词叫作冠词，冠词分定冠词the和不定冠词a, an两类，以元音音素开头的词前用an，以辅音音素开头的词前用a。冠词是应用最广泛的词，也是经常测试的考点之一，并且经常考查它的一些特殊用法。具体使用情况如下。

1. 不定冠词a/an的用法

（1）最基本用法：泛指某一类人、事或物，相当于any。例如：

A horse is a useful animal.

马是有用的动物。

A teacher must love his students.

老师必须爱自己的学生。

（2）泛指某人或某物，不具体说明何人或何物，相当于some。例如：

A gentleman is asking to see you at the school gate.

一位先生要求在学校门口见你。

（3）表示数量"一"，相当于one，但数量概念不是非常强烈。例如：

There is an English-Chinese dictionary on my desk so that I can use it at any time.

我办公桌上有一本英汉词典，以便我随时使用。

（4）表示"每一个"，相当于per or every。例如：

We have forty classes a week and three meals a day.

我们每周四十节课，每天三顿饭。

（5）跟序数词连用表示"又一、再一"，相当于another。例如：

After he failed in the driving test, he determined to practice more and tried **a second** time.

驾照考试失败后，他决心练习更多次并且再考一次。

（6）跟专有名词连用，表示"一个叫……人或物"。例如：

He is always helping others and he is **a living** Lei Feng nowadays.

他总是帮助别人，真是当代活雷锋。

（7）用在抽象名词前表示具体化，往往在名词前面加一个形容词作定语。例如：

I am going to give him **a great** surprise at his birthday party.

我打算在他生日宴会上给他一个大的惊喜。

（8）用于前面加了定语的季节、月份、日期、三餐、世上独一无二的名词前。例如：

He had **a large** and delicious dinner today.

他今天吃了一大顿可口的晚餐。

The accident happened on **a stormy** Sunday last month.

这个事故发生在上个月一个暴风雨的星期天。

China really hopes to have **a peaceful** and friendly world in the 21st century.

中国希望二十一世纪拥有一个和平友好的世界。

（9）经常用在下列短语中：

a lot of 许多   a bit of 一点

a great number of 大量的   a good many 很多

a large amount of 大量   a great deal of 许多

as a result 结果   as a consequence 结果

as a matter of fact 事实上   after a while 过了一会儿

all of a sudden 突然   at a distance 在稍远处

have a cold/a cough/a stomachache/a fever 感冒、咳嗽、胃痛、发高烧

have a dictation 听写

have a rest / a break / a walk 休息、散步

have a look 看看

have a good / bad time 过得好、过得不好

have a word with sb 和某人说句话　　get a word in 插话

take an interest in 对······感兴趣　　take a bath 洗澡

make a face 做鬼脸　　make a living 谋生

make a contribution to 贡献　　once upon a time 从前

once in a while 偶尔　　in a hurry 匆忙地

in a word 一句话

2. 定冠词the的用法

（1）最基本用法：特指某人、某物、某些人、某些物。例如：

This is **the** mobile phone that I bought last week.

这是我上周买的那部手机。

（2）指谈话者双方都知道的人或事。例如：

Close **the** door，please! It is noisy outside.

请关上门! 外面很吵闹。

（3）一个名词第一次被提到用不定冠词，第二次被提到用定冠词。例如：

There is **an** old car in the courtyard. **The** car is beyond repair.

院子里有一辆旧车。那辆车已无法修理。

（4）指世界上独一无二的东西。例如：

The earth goes around **the** sun without stopping day and night.

地球日夜不停地绕着太阳转。

（5）用在序数词和形容词最高级之前。例如：

This is **the** first time that I have visited **the** longest bridge in the world.

这是我第一次参观世界上最长的大桥。

（6）用在由两个以上的普通名词构成的专有名词之前。例如：

Hopefully，I will have a chance to visit **the** United States of America.

希望我有机会参观一下美利坚合众国。

（7）和形容词连用表示一类人。例如：

The rich lives in luxurious surroundings.

富人生活在奢侈的环境中。

（8）用在单数名词前表示一类事物。例如：

The horse is a useful animal. = A horse is a useful animal.

马是有用的动物。

（9）经常用于表示方位的介词短语中。例如：

He is standing under the tree in the west of the school.

他站在学校西边的树下面。

（10）用在姓氏复数名词前表示"一家人"或"两口子"。例如：

The Smiths are watching a live program on TV.

史密斯一家正在看一个电视直播节目。

（11）用在发明物名词之前。例如：

Edison invented the light bulb，which brought convenience to people's life.

爱迪生发明了电灯泡，这给人们的生活带来了便利。

（12）用在乐器名词之前，但在中国传统乐器前不用。例如：

She liked playing the piano and I liked playing erhu when we were at school.

上学时，她喜欢弹钢琴而我喜欢拉二胡。

（13）用在表示江、河、湖、海、运河以及海湾、海峡、山脉、群岛等名词之前。例如：

The Yangtze River is the longest and the Yellow River is the second longest in China.

长江是中国第一长河，黄河位居第二。

（14）比较级中用定冠词的两种句式：第一，"越……越……"；第二，"两者中更……的一个"。例如：

The longer we stay here，the more we want to stay.

我们在这儿待得越久就越想待下去。

There are two boys standing on the playground. The taller is my younger brother.

操场上站着两个男孩。个头高的那位是我弟弟。

（15）用在表示"打、击、抓、牵"等及物动词+ somebody+介词+the，身体部位中。例如：

The teacher hit me on the head slightly when I was absent in the class.

当我在课堂上心不在焉时，老师轻轻敲打我的头。

（16）用在年代、世纪、时期或朝代前。例如：

It was in the 1990's，when he was in his fifties，he actively participated in some social activities.

20世纪90年代，当他五十多岁时，他还积极参加一些社会活动。

（17）用在by加计量的可数名词前。例如：

She was paid by the hour at that time but now she is paid by the month.

那时候她是按小时获得酬劳，而现在是按月获得酬劳。

（18）用在一些固定短语中：

all the same 仍然	all the time 一直
at the moment 此刻	at the same time 同时
by the way 顺便提一下	on the other hand 另一方面
in the end 最后	in the front of 在……的前部
at the back of 在……的后面	at the end of 在……末端
at the beginning of 在……开始的时候	
in the beginning 起初	
by the end of 到……为止	on the whole 总体上
in the morning / afternoon / evening 在上午、下午、晚上	
in the open air 在户外	go to the cinema 去看电影
all over the country 全国	in the middle of 在……中间
the other day 那天	the day after tomorrow 后天
the day before yesterday 前天	take the place of 代替
in the form of 以……的形式	
on the radio / phone 在收音机 / 电话上	
in the distance 在远处	on the contrary 相反
in the least 丝毫	out of the question 不可能
in the charge of 由……负责	in the control of 受……控制
in the possession of 由……拥有	in the future 未来
the two of us 咱俩	

3. 零冠词的情况

（1）用在专有名词和不可数名词前。例如：

Cotton is mainly produced in **Xinjiang China**.

棉花主要在中国新疆出产。

（2）复数名词表示一类人或物时。例如：

Horses are useful animals and they like eating green leaves.

马是有用的动物，它们喜欢吃绿色的叶子。

（3）用在没有修饰语的星期、月份、季节及一些节日前。例如：

It is quite hot on **Children's Day** in summer and very cold on **Christmas Day** in winter.

夏天过儿童节时天相当热，而冬天过圣诞节时天很冷。

（4）在表称呼或表头衔、职位的名词作补足语和同位语时。例如：

When were you elected **president** of that university for the first time，Uncle?

叔叔，你第一次当选为那所大学校长是什么时候?

（5）用在学科名称、三餐以及球类运动前。例如：

I like playing **basketball** after **supper**，because it can not only build up my body but also is helpful to my major—physics.

我喜欢晚饭后打篮球，因为这不仅可以强身而且对我的物理学专业也有帮助。

（6）介词by后跟表示交通工具、通信方式或计量单位的抽象名词。例如：

by car / bus / train / bike / truck / plane / boat / ship / motor

by sea / water / air / land / road

by telephone / telegram / e-mail / law

by weight / height / size / width / length

（7）介词in后面跟表语言、颜料或材料的名词。例如：

He keeps a diary **in English** while I keep a diary **in the Chinese language**.（注意区别）

他用英语写日记而我用中文写日记。

She likes writing **in pencil** and I often write **with a pencil**，too.（注意区别）

她喜欢用铅笔写字，我也经常用铅笔写。

（8）用在"名词+介词+名词"的独立主格结构中。例如：

The policeman went into the room，**gun in hand**.

那位警察进了屋子，手里拿着枪。

（9）系动词turn后跟名词作表语时。例如：

After many years' hard work，she finally turned **president** in the school.

努力工作很多年后，她终于成了那所学校的校长。

（10）在as，though引导的倒装让步状语从句中有单数可数名词时。例如：

Child as / though she is，she knows a lot of film and sports stars.

尽管她是个孩子，但她知道好多电影和体育明星。

（11）用在and，after，by，from等连接的成对的名词短语中。例如：

day and night 夜以继日

hand and foot 尽力地

heart and soul 全心全意

husband and wife 夫妻

right and wrong 是非

father and son 父子

mother and daughter 母女

body and soul 全心全意

brother and sister 兄妹

here and there 零星分散，到处

day after day 日复一日

battle after battle 一次次战争

experiment after experiment 一次次实验

test after test 一次次测验

exam after exam 一次接一次考试

little by little 渐渐

year by year 逐年

one by one 一个接一个

step by step 逐渐地

side by side 肩并肩地

bit by bit 一点一点地

from time to time 不时地

from south to north 从南到北

from morning till night 从早到晚

from beginning to end 自始至终

from house to house 挨家挨户

from head to foot 从头到脚

from right to left 从右到左

from mouth to mouth 广泛流传地

shoulder to shoulder 肩并肩

arm in arm 手挽手

hand in hand 手拉手

（12）在一些固定短语中。例如：

at home 在家

at night 在晚上

at noon / dawn / dusk / midnight 在正午 / 黎明 / 黄昏 / 午夜

on foot 步行

on time 准时

in time 及时

at work 在上班

in class 在上课

on duty 值日

on show 展览

take pride in 以……为傲

go home / to school / to bed / to work 回家 / 上学 / 睡觉 / 上班

go shopping / swimming / fishing / running 去购物 / 游泳 / 钓鱼 / 跑步

take care of 照顾

sentence sb to death 判处某人死刑

make progress 取得进步

make room for 为……腾地

come into action 投入战斗

in silence 默默地

in sight / out of sight 看见 / 看不见

in doubt 不确定

in case（of）万一

in / out of place 在 / 不在适当的地方

in other words 换句话说

in surprise 惊讶地

in bed 卧床

in future 从今往后

at table 在吃饭

on earth 到底

in possession of 拥有

put it into practice 付诸实践

pay attention to 注意

make use of 利用

come into use 开始被使用

come into being 产生

in common 共同

in public 公开地

in debt 负债

in place of 代替

in use 使用中

in / out of trouble 陷入 / 摆脱困境

in charge of 负责

in office 执政

in secret 秘密地

leave school 辍学

out of question 毫无疑问

take possession of 拥有

go to sea / prison / college 航海 / 坐牢 / 上大学

二、数词

1. 基数词

表示数量多少的词叫作基数词。13～19的基数词以-teen结尾，20～90的整十位数的基数词以-ty结尾。

（1）十位和个位之间要加连字符"-"，百位和十位之间加and。例如：

Our company has sold one million two hundred twenty thousand three hundred and fifty-five books.

我们公司已经卖了一百二十二万零三百五十五本书。

（2）把基数词放在dozen，score，hundred，thousand，million，billion等词前表示具体数目时，这些词后不加-s，直接跟名词，但score后可以加of。例如：

He has bought **two dozen eggs and two score of apples**.

他买了两打鸡蛋和四十个苹果。

（3）在dozen，score，hundred，thousand，million，billion等词前面不加具体基数词，表示笼统数目时，要在这些词后加-s，也可在前面加several，few，some，many等词。例如：

Tens of hundreds of students will enter for the college entrance exams.

数以万计的学生将报名参加大学入学考试。

There are **several** thousands of students having a meeting on the playground.

有几千学生在操场上开会。

（4）用于年、月、日，时刻表达法以及"第几……"的表达法等。

On May 10th，2021，we learned Unit Five of Module Seven.

= On 10th of May，2021，we learned Unit Five of Module Seven.

2021年五月十日，我们学习了模块七的第五单元。

In the 1990's，when he was in his thirties，he went abroad for further study.

在20世纪90年代，当他三十多岁时，他出国深造了。

It's ten past five. 五点过十分。（30分以内习惯上用"分+past +时"）

It's ten to five. 五点差十分。（30分以上习惯上用"分+ to+下一个时"）

It's six twenty. 六点二十分。（任何情况下都可以"先说时，后说分"）

It's six fifty. 六点五十分。

2. 序数词

表示顺序的词叫作序数词，每个基数词都有自己的序数词，一般是在基数词后加-th构成，-ty结尾的基数词变y为-i，再加-eth。序数词一般与定冠词the连用。例如：

You will be **the twentieth** to make a speech at the meeting tomorrow.

明天在会上你第二十个发言。

The fifth unit will be learned in **the twelfth** week.

第五单元将在第十二周学习。

Who came out **first** in the Beijing Olympic men's 100-meter race?   （first 用作
副词，不加冠词）

北京奥运会男子100米谁第一名?

He wanted to have **a third** cake because **the second** one he ate was too small.（a
third = another）

他想再吃块蛋糕，因为他吃的第二块太小。

3. 分数及百分数

分子用基数词，分母用序数词，当分子大于1时，分母序数词后加-s；百分
数由基数词加percent构成，percent 永远用单数。例如:

What is **one-third** plus **two-thirds**?

三分之一加三分之二等于多少?

Ninety-nine percent of the students in the school know the fact that more than
seventy percent of the earth's surface is covered by water.

学校百分之九十九的学生知道百分之七十以上的地球表面被水覆盖。

Exercise Five

（一）单句语法填空

1. If we sit near_____ front of the bus, we'll have_____better view.

2. If you go by_____train, you can have quite a comfortable journey, but make
sure you get_____fast one.

3. Two_____（three）of the rivers here have been polluted.

4. This area experienced _____heaviest rainfall in_____month of May.

5. In order to find_____better job, he decided to study_____second foreign language.

6. I know you don't like_____ music very much. But what do you think of
_____ music in the film we saw yesterday?

7. It's _____good feeling for people to admire the Shanghai World Expo that
gives them _____pleasure.

8. The village is far away from here indeed. It's_____four hours' walk.

9. _____twenty-fifth of December is _____Christmas Day.

10. —Hello, could I speak to Mr. Smith?

—Sorry, wrong number. There isn't_____ Mr. Smith here.

（二）单句改错

1. According to World Health Organization, health care plans are needed everywhere to prevent the spread of COVID-19.

2. I can't remember when exactly the Robinsons left the city. I only remember it was the Monday.

3. It took us quite a long time to get here. It was three-hour journey.

4. At a rough estimate, Nigeria is three times size of Great Britain.

5. In the most countries, a university degree can give you a flying start in life.

6. Shortly after the accident, two dozen of police were sent to the spot to keep order.

7. After dinner he gave the Mr. Richardson a ride to the Capital Airport.

8. He is only one of the students who has been a winner of scholarship for three years.

9. He moved to Germany in his sixty.

10. I don't think the experiment is failure. At least we have gained experience.

（三）语法填空

阅读下面材料，在空白处填入适当的冠词，零冠词请打"/"。

Dear Peter,

I'm glad to receive your letter asking for my advice on how to learn___1___ Chinese well. Here are___2___few suggestions. First, it is important to take ___3___Chinese course, so you will be able to learn from___4___teacher and practice with your fellow students. Then, it also helps to watch TV and read___5___books, newspapers and magazines in___6___Chinese whenever possible. Besides, it should be___7___good idea to learn and sing___8___Chinese songs, because by doing so you'll learn and remember Chinese words more easily. You can also make more Chinese friends. They will tell you___9___lot about China and help you. Please write to me in Chinese___10___next time.

（四）短文改错

Last Saturday, some of my friends and I went to the local park for the walk. I saw a elderly woman collecting rubbish thrown by the people. She obviously had any difficulty collecting small things. Suddenly, I came up with the idea. Why not ask my friends to help her collect rubbish? Much to my surprise, both my friends agreed and were willing to help. So we worked hard together with her and collected many rubbish. At an end of this activity, we said goodbye to her. Feeling tired, we walked slowly. After about thirtieth minutes, I got home. I was really happy. I think we'l have a beautiful society if all people help each other. What meaningful day!

第六章 介词和连词

一、介词

介词是英语中的一种虚词，也可叫作前置词，表示词与词之间的某种关系，介词不能单独作句子成分。在学习中重点掌握介词的用法和区别以及介词跟名词、形容词和动词的搭配等。

1. 介词的种类

（1）简单介词：in，on，to，with，by，for，at，about，between，before，after，among，beyond等。

（2）合成介词：into，onto，within，without，throughout，inside，outside等。

（3）短语介词：according to，because of，instead of，due to，in spite of，owing to，in front of，thanks to，other than，apart from，as to，as for，but for，in addition to，in case of，on account of，in comparision of，in connection with等。

（4）分词介词：including，considering，regarding，concerning等。

2. 介词短语的作用

首先要明确短语介词与介词短语的概念区别，短语介词是以短语形式出现的复杂介词（如：according to，because of，instead of等），而介词短语则是介词和名词、代词、动名词、数词、不定式以及宾语从句构成的一个短语，通常在句中可以作表语、定语、状语以及宾语补足语。例如：

All of them are **in front of the teaching building.**（介词短语作表语）

他们都在教学楼前面。

The girls **in red skirts** are from a famous university of China. （介词短语作定语）

那些穿红裙子的女孩来自中国的一所名牌大学。

There are a lot of valuable trees **in our schoolyard**. （介词短语作状语）

我们学校院子里有许多珍贵树木。

Who left the basketball **on the playground**? （介词短语作宾补）

谁把篮球丢在操场上了?

3. 介词的基本用法

（1）表示时间的介词有：in, at, on, for, since, by, before, after, until等。

in用在世纪、朝代、年代、年、季节、月份、一段时间之前以及in the morning / afternoon / evening中。

at用在时刻、一段时间的节假日之前以及at night中。

on用在具体的某一天或某一天的上午、下午、晚上之前。

for后接一段时间，整个短语与延续性动词连用。

since后接具体时间，整个短语多与完成时态连用。

by表示"不迟于……"，相当于not later than。

before后多跟表时间点的名词，after后既可跟时间点也可跟时间段的名词。

until后接时间点，表示动作"持续到……"，多与not连用。例如：

in the 18th century, in Tang Dynasty, in the 1880s, in 2013, in autumn, in December, in an hour, in a while, in no time

at half past six, at dawn, at daybreak, at noon, at dusk, at midnight, at night, at the weekend, at Christmas, at the Spring Festival

on September 10th, on Sunday, on the early morning of December 16th, on Christmas Day

He has been whitewashing the walls **for five hours**.

他持续刷墙有五个小时了。

He has taught English in this school **since 1982**.

他自1982年以来一直在这所学校教英语。

You'd better come back home for supper **by six o'clock p.m.**

你最好在下午六点以前回家吃晚饭。（不迟于六点）

We had produced more than ten thousand washing machines **by the end** of last year.

到去年年底为止我们已经生产了一万多台洗衣机。

I'll be back **before nine** o'clock p.m.

我晚上九点以前就回来了。

She went to Japan **after a month.**=She went to Japan **a month later**.

一个月以后她去了日本。

I'll be free **after six** o'clock p.m. and then I will come to see you.

下午六点以后我就有空了，那时我将过来看你。

He **didn't** go to bed **until 12** o'clock at midnight.

他直到午夜十二点才去睡觉。

（2）表示方位的介词有：at, on, in, to, above, below, over, under, in front of, in the front of, between, among, towards, from, out of, for, across, through, by等。

at用于较小的地方，门牌号等之前。

on表示"在……表面上"、"与……接壤"、"树上的果实"、打在人体较硬的地方等。

in用在较大的地方之前，也表示在某范围内，打在人体肉较多的地方等。

to表示在某范围以外，"朝着……"= towards。

above, below, over, under（用法见"四、易混介词辨析"中的2、3）。

in front of在某范围外的前面，in the front of在某范围内的前部。

between 表示在两者之间，among表示在三者以上之间。

from强调"从某个起点"，而out of强调"从……里面出来"。

for表示动身去某地。

across, through, by, past的用法见"四、易混介词辨析"中的6。例如：

She lives **at** Green Street 102 and we are supposed to meet **at** the bus stop near her home.

她住在格林街102号，我们预期在她家附近的公共汽车站见面。

Vietnam lies **on** the south of China.

越南与中国南部接壤。

There are more apples on the tree this year than last year.

今年这棵树上结得苹果比去年多。

He hit me on the head / forehead / nose / ear / neck / shoulder / leg / back.

他打在我的头（额头、鼻子、耳朵、脖子、肩膀、腿部、背）上。

She has lived in Hongkong for 20 years，which lies in the south of China.

她已经在位于中国南部的香港住了20年了。

The dead bird in the tree fell down and hit him in the face / eye / mouth / chest / stomach.

树上的那只死鸟掉下来，砸在他的脸（眼睛、嘴巴、胸部及腹部）上。

Hebei Province lies to the northwest of Shanghai.

河北省位于上海西北部。

Finally she rose and walked slowly to / towards me.

最后她站起来，慢慢朝我走来。

He had a different attitude towards machines，which resulted in some inventions of machinery.

他对机器有着不同的态度，这就导致了一些机械的发明。

There is a small river running in front of my house.

我的房子前面有一条小河流过。

The driver drives the bus sitting in the front of it.

司机坐在公共汽车前部开着车。

The tall man is standing between two high buildings.

那个高个子男人站在两栋高楼之间。

There are a lot of fallen apples on the ground among the trees.

地上那些树之间有许多掉下来的苹果。

The airplane from Shanghai will land on our airport in 20 minutes.

那架来自上海的飞机20分钟后降落在我们机场。

The students came out of the classroom one by one after the bell rang.

铃响之后，学生们一个接一个地从教室里走出来。

Early in the morning we set out for our destination on business.

一大早我们就动身去目的地出差。

4. 易混介词辨析

（1）about & on

这两个介词都表"关于"，但意义不同，about表示的内容较为普通，而on一般表示较为严肃的或者学术性的问题，指可供专门领域的人阅读和研究的内容。例如：

This is a book **about** American history.

这是一本关于美国历史的书。

In one of his books，Marx gave some advice **on** how to learn a foreign language.

马克思在一本书里提出了关于如何学外语的一些建议。

（2）above，on & over

这三个介词都表示"在……上"，above表示"高于……"，物体之间不接触。

on强调"在……表面上"，物体之间有接触。

over表示"在……垂直上方"，还有"覆盖"和"遍及"之意。例如：

The temperature will stay **above** zero in the daytime.

白天气温保持在零度以上。

The picture of the great scientist is **above** the blackboard.

那位伟大科学家的画挂在黑板上方。

There are many textbooks **on** the desk.

课桌上有许多教科书。

There was an electric light **over** the table.

课桌上方有一盏电灯。

He put his jacket **over** the child.

他把他的夹克衫盖在孩子身上。

The story soon spread all **over** the city and even all **over** the country.

这个故事很快传遍整个城市乃至全国。

（3）below & under

这两个介词均表示"在……之下"，below表示位置低于某物或在下方，不一定在正下方，还可以指价值、地位、等级、温度等"低于……"。

under表示"在……正下方"，还可以指在某人"领导、管理、统治之下"。例如：

Did you see the boat **below** the bridge?

你看见桥下的船了吗？

The temperature today is 10 degrees **below** zero.

今天的气温在零下十度。

The teacher entered the classroom with a thick book **under** his arm.

老师走进教室，腋下夹着一本厚厚的书。

Under the wise leadership of the Communist Party of China, we are marching forward proudly.

在中国共产党的英明领导下，我们正阔步前进。

（4）by，in & with

这三个介词均表示"用"，by后跟动名词或名词，表示以某种方式做事，后跟交通工具时不加冠词。

in后跟名词，表示以某种语言、方式等，后跟交通工具时可加冠词和其他修饰语。

with后跟名词，表示用某种工具或器官等。例如：

Everybody earns their living **by** selling something.

每个人都是以卖某东西来谋生。

We will go to Hong Kong **by** plane tomorrow.

我们明天坐飞机去香港。

An English teacher should try to teach his lessons **in** English.

英语老师应该用英语授课。

You shouldn't have treated the matter **in** the wrong way.

你不应该以错误的方式对待这件事。

You'd better not write **with** a pencil.

你最好不要用铅笔写。

Human beings walk **with** their legs and see **with** their eyes.

人用腿走路，用眼睛看东西。

（5）in & after

这两个介词均表示"过……后"，in后接表时间段的名词，用在含有短暂性动词的将来时态的句子中，表示"在将来一段时间之后"动作就发生。

after后接表时间段的名词时，用于一般过去时的句子中，表示"在过去一段时间后"动作发生，也可用在一般将来时的句子中，后跟表时间点的名词，表示"在某个时刻之后"动作将发生。例如：

He will come back **in two hours**.

两个小时之后他就回来了。

He left for Beijing **after three days**.

三天之后他动身去北京了。

He will leave for Beijing **after two o'clock**.

两点以后他动身去北京。

（6）across，through，over，by & past

以上介词均表示"穿过"，across表示从某个表面"穿过"，与介词on相关。

through多指从某物中间"穿过"，与介词in相关。

over指从某物上面"翻越"。

by指从某人或某物旁边"经过"。

past强调从某事物的一旁经过。例如：

You will find the hospital right **across** the square.

医院就在广场的正对面。

The policeman forced his way **through** the crowd.

警察从人群中穿过。

I don't think anyone can jump **over** the fence.

我认为任何人都不能翻越那个栅栏。

He walked **by** me without saying a word.

他一声没吭地从我身边走过。

When our bus drove **past** the Tian'anmen Square，all the people cheered.

当我们的公共汽车驶过天安门广场时，大家都欢呼了。

（7）at，in，with，for & over

以上介词均与表示喜、怒、哀、乐、恐惧、惊讶等的动词或者形容词连用，表示情感方面的原因、理由或动机。

at表示听到某个消息、看到某个情景、得到某个报告等，常跟angry，surprised，pleased，frightened，excited，cheer连用。

in常跟在joy，delight，take pleasure，show interest，take pride之后。

with常跟在表示身体动作的动词和表示状态的形容词之后。

for后接表示感情的抽象名词，意为"由于……""对……"。

over通常跟在表示感情的动词cry，weep，laugh等之后，表示"针对……"。例如：

At the news they were very surprised and then frightened.

听到这个消息时，他们既惊讶又害怕。

Mr. Smith delights in helping others.

史密斯先生以助人为乐。

The teacher was not satisfied with my answer and shook his head with anger.

老师对我的答案不满意，并且生气地摇了一下头。

He didn't go to sleep for excitement last night.

他昨晚兴奋得不能入睡。

They all laughed over the joke during the class yesterday.

昨天他们就那个笑话笑了一节课。

（8）except，besides，except for，but，other than & apart from

上述介词均表示"除了"，但用法不同。

except表示"除了……不包括在内"的意思，后面也可以跟that，when，where引导的宾语从句，在句首时可用except for代替。

besides表示"除……以外，还有"，句中经常有other，else，also，another等暗示词。

except for表示除去一个细节或一个内容来修正前面所叙述的内容。

but多与否定意义的词连用，也可以和except换用，后面还可以跟动词不定式，但but前面有了do的任何形式，后面的to都要省略。

other than就是"除了……不包括在内"，意思同except。

apart from 既可以用作besides，也可以用作except，还可以用作except for。例如：

We have classes every day **except** Sunday, on which we usually go home.

除了星期天，我们每天都有课，星期天我们通常就回家了。

The suit is quite good **except** that the trousers are a little longer.

除了裤子有点长，这套衣服很好。

He never comes to see me **except** when he is in need of help.

除了需要帮助，他从不来看我。

She drove to all the places **except** where cars couldn't reach.

她开车去了所有的地方，除了车子不能到达的（地方）。

Except for the desk, everything is in order.= Everything is in order **except** the desk.

除了桌子，一切都很整齐。

He can speak several other languages **besides** his native tongue.

除了母语，他还会说其他几种语言。

The temple is quite empty **except for** a monk.

那座庙里除了一个和尚空空无也。

He had nothing in the world **but** a million pound note.

在这个世界上，除了一张百万英镑的票子他什么都没有。

The animal has no choice **but to** lie down and sleep when winter comes.

=The animal has nothing **to do but** lie down and sleep when winter comes.

冬天来了，这个动物除了躺下来睡觉别无选择。

The form cannot be signed by anyone **other than** yourself.

除了你自己，这个表谁都不能签名。

Apart from my students, I have no one to talk to.

除了我的学生，我没有人说话。

Apart from other considerations, time is also a factor.

除了别的考虑，时间也是一个因素。

The composition is quite good **apart from** a few spelling mistakes.

除了一些拼写错误，这篇作文写得很好。

（9）as & like

这两个介词均有"像……一样"之意，as作为介词讲，意为"作为……且本来就是……"，而like是"像……但不是……"的意思。例如：

As a teacher, he treats every student equally and well.

作为老师，他公平地、很好地对待每个学生。

He treats me **like** a father, though he is my brother.

尽管他是我哥哥，但他对待我就像父亲一样。

（10）of & for

这两个介词引出动词不定式逻辑主语时用法不同，当形容词（kind，good，nice，clever，stupid，foolish，polite，cruel，typical，etc）说明不定式逻辑主语的品质特征时用of；当形容词（important，necessary，possible，strange，natural，etc）说明不定式的性质时用for。例如：

It is very kind **of** you to help those poor people. =You are very kind to help those poor people.

你帮助那些穷人，你真好。

It is very important **for** you to read English aloud for at least 20 minutes every morning.

每天早晨朗读至少二十分钟的英语是非常重要的。

5. 常见介词搭配

（1）与at搭配的短语。

at dawn 在黎明	at daybreak 在破晓
at noon 在正午	at dusk 在黄昏
at midnight 在午夜	at night 在夜间
at sunrise 在日出时	at sunset 在日落时
at table 在吃饭	at school 在上学
at college 在上大学	at home 在家
at present 目前	at the moment 此刻
at that time 那时	at risk 冒险
at first 起初	at the beginning of 在开始的时候
at the end of 在结束的时候、在末端	at the sight of 看见
be good / clever / expert at 擅长	at the mercy of 在……掌控中
be angry / annoyed / surprised at 对……生气 （恼火、惊讶）	

（2）与in搭配的短语。

in a hurry 匆忙	in a low voice 低声地
in high spirits 情绪高涨	in low / poor spirits 情绪低落
in tears 含泪地	in fear 恐惧地
in danger 在危险中	in silence 静静地
in good health 身体好	in bad health 身体不好
in public 公开地	in doubt 疑问中
in time 及时	in flower 开花
in black 穿着黑衣服	in rags 穿着破衣服
in trouble 在麻烦中	in need 需要
in surprise 惊讶地	in good condition 状态好
in a good state 状态好	in every（all）direction（s）朝四面八方
in search of 搜寻	in one's search for 搜寻
in honor of 纪念 / 给某人荣誉	in memory of 纪念
be dressed in 穿着	be engaged in 忙于
differ in 在……方面不同	be interested in 对……感兴趣
do well in 在某方面做得好	
be rich（poor）in 在某方面丰富（缺乏）	

（3）与from搭配的短语。

from house to house 挨家挨户	from beginning to end 从头至尾
far from 远离	be different from 不同于
be free from 免受	
prevent/stop/keep sb.from 阻止某人做某事	
protect / defend / guard / save sb. from doing 保护某人不受侵害	
distinguish from 不同于	differ from 不同于
separate from 分开	

（4）与to搭配的短语。

the access to 进入	the approach to 入口
the way to 去……的路	the key to 关键是（在于）
the answer to ……的答案	the visit to 访问

the notes to ……的注释

the response to 对……的反应

the bridge to 通向……的桥梁

the danger to ……的危险

（以上四个短语中的to均表示"……的"。）

pay attention to 注意

devote ……to 致力于

be equal to 平等

be married to 和某人结婚

be familiar to 为……所熟悉

be faithful to 对某人忠诚

be contrary to 与……相反

be kind / good / bad / cruel / rude to sb. 对某人友善、好、坏、冷酷、粗鲁

（5）与with搭配的短语。

be angry with 对某人生气

be annoyed with 对某人恼火

be familiar with 对……熟悉

be strict with 对某人严格

be busy with 忙于

be patient with 对……有耐心

be popular with 受某人喜欢

with speed 迅速地

with a sneer 轻蔑地

with a sigh 唉声叹气地

with a smile 微笑地

with difficulty 困难地、吃力地

（6）与of搭配的短语。

lacking of 缺乏

be ashamed of 害羞

be aware of 意识到

be fond of 喜欢

be afraid of 害怕

for fear of 唯恐

for the sake of 为了……的缘故

in time of 在……的时刻

in charge of 负责

in the charge of 由……负责

in possession of 拥有

in the possession of 由……拥有

in control of 控制

in the control of 由……控制

be made up of 由……组成

be composed of 由……组成

consist of 由……组成

be informed of 通知

rob sb. of sth. 抢劫

cure sb. of sth 治疗

be convinced of 说服

cheat sb. of 欺骗

suspect sb. of 怀疑

warn sb. of 警告

（7）与on搭配的短语。

on behalf of 代表

have an effect / influence on 对……有影响

have mercy on 同情

once upon a time 从前

get on / along with 与某人相处

look down on 看不起

hold on to 留着不卖

congratulate sb. on sth 祝贺某人某事

call on 号召、拜访

drop in on 顺便拜访

look on as 看作

depend / rely on 依靠

二、连词的定义、分类及用法

连词是一种虚词，用来连接词与词、短语与短语、句子与句子，不能单独充当句子成分，只起连接作用。按照语法作用分为并列连词、从属连词和连接代（副）词。

1. 并列连词

我们通常把用来连接词与词、短语与短语、分句与分句的词叫作并列连词，常见的并列连词有：and，but，or，so，when，both...and，not only...but also...，as well as，either...or...，neither...nor...，not...but...，for，while，etc。例如：

Study hard and you will be sure to succeed sooner or later.

努力学习，总有一天你会成功的。

He doesn't smoke now but he did twenty years ago.

他现在不抽烟，但二十年前抽。

Watch carefully，or you will probably have difficulty in doing it yourselves.

认真观察，否则你们自己做的时候会有困难的。

There were no taxis in the street，so we had to walk home in the rain.

街上没有出租车了，所以我们不得不淋着雨走回家。

I was walking in the street when a terrible earthquake happened. （when=and at this time suddenly）

我正在街上走着，突然可怕的地震发生了。

I was just about to go to bed when someone knocked at the door.

我正打算睡觉，这个时候有人敲门。

I had just gone to bed when the telephone rang in the sitting-room.

我刚上床睡觉，客厅里的电话铃就响了。

Both my father **and** mother are retired workers **and** healthy now.

我的爸爸妈妈都是退休工人并且身体健康。

Not only is he interested in action movies **but also** his family are fond of watching them.

不仅他对动作片感兴趣，而且他的家人也喜欢看。

The teacher, **as well as** his students is going to Qinhuangdao for a holiday. （就远一致）

这位老师和他的学生一起去秦皇岛度假。

Either you **or** I am mad. （就近一致）

不是你疯了就是我疯了。

Neither the teacher **nor** the students are on the playground. （就近一致）

老师和学生都不在操场。

She is **not** a lower-class woman, **but** an upper-class lady with a lot of money.

她不是下层社会妇女，而是上层社会阔太太。

The electric current must have been turned off, **for** the light went out.

一定是停电了，因为灯灭了。

He is tall **and** strong **while** his wife is very short **and** thin.

他又高又壮，而他妻子又矮又瘦。

2. 从属连词

我们通常把用来引导状语从句的词叫作从属连词。常见的从属连词有：

（1）表时间：when, while, as, whenever, since, once, until, till, as soon as, after, before, no sooner...than..., hardly...when..., the moment, the minute, the instant, the second, immediately, directly, instantly, every time, each time, the first time, the last time, by the time, next time, the time, the day, the week, the year, etc。

（2）表地点：where, wherever, anywhere, everywhere, etc。

（3）表条件：if, unless, as long as, so long as, suppose, supposing, in case, on condition that, providing that, provided that, etc。

（4）表让步：though, although, while, as, even if, even though, no matter what, whatever, no matter who, whoever, no matter which, whichever, no matter whom，whomever，no matter when，whenever，no matter how，however，no matter where，wherever，etc。

（5）表原因：because，as，since，now that，etc。

（6）表比较：than，as...as，not so... as，etc。

（7）表目的：so that，in order that，etc。

（8）表结果：so... that，such... that，so that，in case，for fear that，etc。

（9）表方式：as，as if，as though，etc。

（有关从属连词用法见"状语从句"一章。）

3. 连接代词和连接副词

我们通常把用来引导名词性从句的词叫作连接代（副）词。常见的有三类：

（1）that 没有词义，不做句子成分，只起连接作用。

（2）whether / if 意思为"是否"，不做句子成分，起连接作用。

（3）what，whatever，which，whichever，who，whoever，whom，whomever，when，whenever，where，wherever，how，however，why，etc。有词义，作句子成分，起连接作用。

（有关连接代词和副词的用法见"名词性从句"一章。）

4. 连词however，wherever，whenever，whatever，whoever等的用法

however既可引导让步状语从句、名词性从句，也可以用作疑问代词和疑问副词等。

（1）引导让步状语从句时等于no matterhow。例如：

However late you are，we will wait for you to have dinner together.

=No matter how late you are，we will wait for you to have dinner together.

无论你回来的有多么晚，我们都会等你一起吃晚饭。

Wherever / No matter where you go，I will follow you.

无论你去哪里，我都会跟着你。

Whenever it is convenient to you，please come to my office.

= No matter when it is convenient to you，please come to my office.

无论何时方便，请来我办公室一下。

Whatever you do，I will support you forever.

= No matter what you do，I will support you forever.

无论你做什么，我都永远支持你。

Whoever the injured are，I would donate this money to them.

= No matter who the injured are，I would donate this money to them.

无论受伤者是谁，我都会把这笔钱捐给他们。

（2）引导名词性从句时只能用Wherever。例如：

Wherever he will go to Beijing hasn't been decided yet.

他到底怎么去北京还没有决定下来。

Wherever and whenever the interview will be held is still a secret.

面试到底什么时候在哪里举行还是个秘密。

Whatever you say is right and reasonable.

无论你说什么都是对的，并且合乎道理。

Whoever breaks the regulation should be punished.

无论谁违反此规定都应该受到处罚。

（3）Wherever仍然用作疑问代词和疑问副词，用来加强语气。例如：

Wherever tall is the huge man over there?

那边的那个巨人到底有多高？

Wherever do these girls want to have their picnic?

这些女孩子到底想去哪里野餐？

Whenever are you going to invite us to attend your wedding?

你打算到底什么时候请我们参加你的婚礼？

Whatever do you want to say in such a case?

在这种情况下你想说什么呢？

Whoever will come to teach us English instead of Mr. Yang?

到底谁来替杨先生教我们英语？

Exercise Six

（一）单句语法填空

1. Start out right away_____ you'll miss the first train.

2. It is reported that the United States uses twice_____much energy as the whole of Europe.

3. Scientists are convinced of the positive effect of laughter_____physical and mental health.

4. In case_____fire, all exits must be kept clear.

5. Most of us know we should cut down on fat, but knowing such things isn't much help when it comes_____shopping and eating.

6. There is no such thing_____a free lunch, so eventually they'll figure out how to pass on the coat to the customers.

7. This new model of car is so expensive that it is_____the reach of those with average incomes.

8. I like his speech very much, because it was clear and _____ the point.

9. John became a football coach in Sealion Middle School_____the beginning of March.

10. Many people who had seen the film were afraid to go to the forest when they remembered the scenes _____ which people were eaten by the tiger.

（二）单句改错

1. I always take something to read when I go to the doctor's in case of I have to wait.

2. Roses need special care so as they can live through winter.

3. Parents should take seriously their children's requests for sunglasses though eye protection is necessary in sunny weather.

4. The cost of living in Glasgow is among the lowest in Britain when the quality of life is probably one of the highest.

5. People try to avoid public transportation delays by using their own cars and this by turn creates further problems.

6. Many Chinese universities provided scholarships for students in need financial aid.

7. With time went on, Einstein's theory proved to be correct.

8. I recognized his voice at the moment he spoke.

9. No sooner had she told her the bad news that she burst into tears.

10. He got to the station early for fear missing his train.

（三）语法填空

阅读下面材料，在空白处填入适当的内容（1个单词）或括号内单词的正确形式。

My dear grandson, your mother told me __1__ you started smoking some time ago and now you are finding it difficult __2__ give it up. By the way, do you know that is __3__ you become addicted in three different ways? Firstly, you can become physically addicted __4__ nicotine, which is one of the hundreds __5__ harmful chemicals in cigarettes. This means that after a while your body becomes accustomed __6__ having nicotine in it. So, __7__ the drug leaves your body, you get withdrawal symptoms. I remember feeling bad-tempered and sometimes even in pain. Secondly, you become addicted through habit. __8__ you know, if you do the same thing over and over again, you begin to do it automatically. Lastly, you can become mentally addicted. When I was young, I believed I was happier __9__ more relaxed after having a cigarette, so I began to think I could only feel good when I smoked. I was addicted in all three ways, so it was very difficult to quit. __10__ I did finally manage.

（四）短文改错

Dear sir,

I'm terribly sorry to make you disappointed for not having finished my homework at time. As a matter in fact, I had something else to do, which made me have no time to my homework.

My father was seriously injured by a car accident yesterday. Before I heard the news, I hurried to the hospital. I had a busy night, but I didn't do my homework.

As you know, I am an ordinary student in class and want to improve my English. I find I have great difficulty on paying attention in my study. Would you please give me some suggestions? Beside, I wish you could give me more chances to practice my English in class.

I'm looking forward to hear from you soon.

Yours sincerely

Li Hwe

第七章　动词及动词短语

关于动词和动词短语，我们要重点掌握动词词义辨析、动词短语辨析、动词搭配、动词的不规则变化等。尤其要注意动词与不同介词和副词构成的短语及其用法。

一、动词的定义及种类

表示动作、状态或者性质的词叫作动词。动词可以分为四类：

（1）行为动词——表示行为或状态的词，可以单独作谓语，行为动词又分为及物动词和不及物动词，不及物动词后不能跟宾语，也没有被动语态。

（2）系动词—— 一般带有表语才会有完整的意义，才能构成谓语。

（3）情态动词——表示说话人对某一动作或状态的态度，不能单独作谓语，后跟动词原形。

（4）助动词——没有词义，不能单独作谓语，常常帮助动词构成不同时态或者否定、疑问等形式。

二、动词的形式

除原形以外，动词还有第三人称单数、-ing形式（现在分词）、过去式及过去分词等形式。

1. 第三人称单数的构成

（1）一般情况下只加-s，如begin—begins, start—starts, end—ends。

（2）以s，x，ch，sh，o结尾的动词加-es，如kiss—kisses, fix—fixes, watch—watches, wash—washes, go—goes, do—does。

（3）以辅音字母加y结尾的动词，变y为i，再加-es，如study—studies,

tidy—tidies。

2. –ing形式的构成

（1）一般情况下直接加-ing，如read—reading，study—studying，learn—learning。

（2）以辅音字母加不发音的e结尾的动词，去e加-ing，如live—living，make—making。

（3）以重读闭音节结尾，末尾只有一个辅音字母的动词，先双写这一辅音字母，再加-ing，如begin—beginning，cut—cutting，get—getting，hit—hitting，run—running，set—setting，sit—sitting，spit—spitting，stop—stopping，swim—swimming，beg—begging，drop—dropping，fit—fitting，nod—nodding，dig—digging，forget—forgetting，regret—regretting，rid—ridding，quit—quitting，put—putting。

（4）以ie结尾的动词，变ie为y，再加-ing，如lie—lying，die—dying，tie—tying。

3. 过去式及过去分词的构成

（1）一般情况下，直接加-ed，如work—worked，appear—appeared，sound—sounded。

（2）以不发音的e结尾的动词直接加-d，如taste—tasted，live—lived，move—moved。

（3）以辅音字母加y结尾的动词，变y为i再加-ed，如study—studied，carry—carried。

（4）以重读闭音节结尾，末尾只有一个辅音字母的动词，先双写这一辅音字母，再加-ed，如stop—stopped，rob—robbed，nod—nodded，drop—dropped，beg—begged。

4. 不规则动词变化的规律

一般可分为三类：

（1）三种形式完全一样（AAA），如burst/burst/burst，cost/cost/cost，cut/cut/cut，hit/hit/hit，hurt/hurt/hurt，put/put/put，spread/spread/spread，shut/shut/shut，set/set/set，cast/cast/cast，read/read/read，thrust/thrust/thrust，split/split/split，fit/fit/fit，let/let/let。

（2）后两种形式一样（ABB），如meet/met/met，lead/led/led，leave/left/left，keep/kept/kept，mean/meant/meant，feel/felt/felt，send/sent/sent，pay/paid/paid，lose/lost/lost，sell/sold/sold，win/won/won，hold/held/held，lay/laid/laid，catch/caught/caught，lend/lent/lent。

（3）三种形式完全不一样（ABC），如arise/arose/arisen，bear/bore/born，blow/blew/blown，do/did/done，begin/began/begun，fall/fell/fallen，rise/rose/risen，lie/lay/lain，tear/tore/torn，freeze/froze/frozen，drink/drank/drunk，wear/wore/worn，choose/chose/chosen，fly/flew/flown，draw/drew/drawn，drive/drove/drive，swim/swam/swum，eat/ate/eaten，take/took/taken，bite/bit/bitten，shake/shook/shaken。

三、系动词的用法

最常用的系动词就是be，另外还有一些由行为动词转化来的系动词，如appear，seem，look，sound，smell，taste，feel，stay，remain，keep，stand，lie，become，turn，go，grow，fall，come，prove，turn out，etc。系动词后都可以跟形容词作表语，但是在用法上略有不同。例如：

（1）系动词be，become，look，seem，grow，prove，turn out，turn等后还可以跟名词作表语，但turn后跟单数可数名词时，要省略冠词a或an。例如：

After many years he finally **turned president** in this university.

很多年后，他成了这所大学的校长。

（2）系动词be后还可以跟介词短语或者表示地点和位置的副词作表语。例如：

Wherever you go，I will be **right here** waiting for you.

无论你去哪里，我都会在这儿等着你。

（3）系动词look，feel，taste，smell，sound可以跟介词like构成的短语作表语。例如：

The snack **tastes like beef** if you chaw for a long time.

你多嚼一会儿，那个小吃尝起来像牛肉。

（4）系动词be，look，feel，sound，seem可以跟as if引导的表语从句。例如：

It **looks as if** he **were** fifty years old，but actually he is thirty.

他看起来像五十岁了，而事实上才三十岁。

（5）系动词be，seem，appear可以跟that引导的表语从句。例如：

It **seemed that** he disliked the dishes that we had prepared for a long time.

他似乎不喜欢我们准备了好长时间的那些菜肴。

（6）系动词remain可以跟名词、形容词、介词短语、副词、现在分词、过去分词以及动词不定式等形式作表语。例如：

He remains **an ordinary** teacher after so many years' teaching.

教学那么多年之后，他仍然是名普通教师。

He remains **very poor** after so many years' hard work.

那么多年努力工作之后，他仍然很穷。

He remains **in poverty** with the help of the government for some years.

接受了政府几年的帮助下，他仍然处于贫穷中。

He remained **here** waiting for her although it was raining hard.

尽管雨下得很大，他仍然在这儿等着她。

He remained **working** in the fields though all the others had left.

尽管大家都离开了，他仍然在地里干活。

It remains **to be seen** whether the old couple will go abroad for a holiday.

那老两口是否去国外度假还有待于验证。

四、动词短语

1. 动词短语的构成方式

（1）动词+介词：

ask after 问

care for 关心

look after 照顾

break through 突破

（2）动词+副词：

break out 爆发

carry on 进行

give up 放弃

give away 泄露

注意：在动词加副词的短语中，如果人称代词作宾语，一定要把代词放在中间。例如：

He used to smoke a lot，but now he has given it up.

他以前抽很多烟，但现在已经戒了。

He pretended that he hadn't done anything wrong，but the sweat on his forehead gave him away.

他假装没做过任何错事，但额头上的汗水把他出卖了。

（3）动词+名词：

take efforts 努力   take one's time 慢慢来

make repairs 修理

（4）动词+副词+介词：

look down upon 看不起   put up with 忍受

do away with 废除

（5）动词+名词+介词：

take care of 照顾   pay attention to 注意

make use of 利用

（6）be+ 形容词+介词：

be fond of 喜欢   be used to 习惯

be suitable for 适合

2. 常见以动词为中心的短语

（1）以 break 为中心：

break away from 脱离，逃离

break down 分解，瓦解，抛锚，身体垮了

break in 闯进，打断；使顺服

break into 闯入，强行进入，突然开始

break out 爆发，发生；起锚

break the law 违反法律

break the record 破纪录

break one's promise 食言

break up 开垦，破碎；解散，分开；撕毁合同

（2）以catch为中心：

caught sb. doing 发现某人做某事 　　be caught in the rain 被雨淋

catch a bus/train 赶汽车/火车 　　catch a cold 伤风，感冒

catch one's word 听懂某人的话 　　catch sight of 发现，瞥见

catch up with 赶上，追上

（3）以come为中心：

come across 偶尔发现，想起；越过

come along 一道来，陪伴；进步，进展

come back 回来；恢复，复原

come down 倒下，降落，跌落，病倒

come from 来自，起源于，从……产生

come in 进来，进入；获名次

come into being 产生，出现，形成 　　come into power 开始执政，当权

come into use 开始使用 　　come on 上演，开始，赶快，登台

come out 出版，结果是，褪色 　　come to 苏醒，共计，达到

come to an end 终止，结束 　　come to know 开始了解到

come true 实现，成为现实 　　come up 走近；上楼；长出，发芽

（4）以do为中心：

do a good deed 做一件好事 　　do away with 去掉，废除；弄死；浪费

do good to=do sb. good 有益于 　　do harm to=do sb. harm 有害于

do wrong to 做错 　　do one's best 尽某人最大努力

do one's homework 做作业 　　do sb. a favor 帮助某人

do well in 学得不错，干得漂亮 　　do with 和……相处，忍受，处理

do without 不需要，凑合 　　do wonders 创造奇迹

have nothing to do with 与……无关

have something to do with 和……有关

（5）以get为中心：

get about 徘徊，走动，旅行；流传 　　get accustomed to 习惯于

get across 度过，横过；使理解 　　get along 前进，进步；同意；离去

get along with 与……相处 　　get away 离开，逃脱

get back 取回，回来；报复

get down 咽下；写下；使沮丧，使抑郁

get down to 认真对待，着手做　　get familiar with 熟悉

get hold of 获得，取得　　　　　get home 到家

get in 进入，陷入；牵涉　　　　　get off 送走，下车，动身

get on 上车，进步，成功，相处　　get on with 进展；与……相处

get out of 由……出来，避免，退休　　get over 越过，恢复，克服，完成

get ready for 为……做准备　　　　get rid of 除去，去掉；免除，摆脱

get through 到达，完成，通过；及格　　get together 积聚，积累；商谈

get up 起床，起立；研究，钻研　　get used to 习惯于

（6）以give为中心：

give away 赠送，牺牲，泄露，颁发　　give back 归还

give in 屈服，让步，投降　　　　　give off 发出（烟、气味）

give out 分发，公布　　　　　　　give place to 让位于，被……所替代

give rise to 引起，导致；使……发生　　give up 放弃，停止

give way to 让步，退却；屈服于

（7）以look为中心：

look about 四下环顾，查看　　　　look after 照顾，看管

look around 东张西望　　　　　　look at 注视，着眼于

look back 回顾　　　　　　　　　look for 寻找

look down on 俯视，轻视　　　　　look forward to 盼望，期待

look into 窥视，调查，浏览　　　　look like 看起来像

look on 旁观，面向　　　　　　　look out 向外看，注意，当心

look over 从上面看过去，检查

look through 透过……看去，看穿，浏览

look up to 仰望，尊敬

（8）以make为中心：

be made from 由……制成（看不出原材料）

be made of 由……制成（能看出原材料）

be made up of 由……组成　　　　make a fool of 愚弄，欺骗

make a mistake 弄错

make use of 使用，利用

make after 追求，追赶

make sure 确信，把……弄清楚

make contact with 与……接触，与……联系

make for 去向，向……前进；有利于

make friends with 和……交友

make into 把……制成，使……转变为

make much of 重视，理解，赏识

make up one's mind 作出决定

make one's own 当作自己的看待

make oneself at home 随便，别拘束

make out 辨认，理解，填写，开支票

make the best of 尽量利用，极为重视

make up 组成，构成，编造，化妆，补齐

make way for 为……让路，让路于……

（9）以put为中心：

put aside 把……放在一边，搁置，忽视

put away 把……放好，储藏

put back 把……放回原处；驳回

put down 放下，镇压，记下，削减，降落

put forward 提出，拨快（钟表），建议，提倡

put into 把……放入，插入，翻译成

put off 推迟，延期

put on 上演；穿上，带上

put one's heart into 全神贯注，专心致志

put up with 忍受，容忍

put up 举起，挂起；张贴；提名，推荐

（10）以take为中心：

take aback 使吃惊，使惊呆

take a seat 就座

take aim 瞄准，设立目标

take away 拿走，减去；夺去

take...by surprise 出奇制胜

take care of 照顾；处理，对付

take...for 把……当作

take off 脱去，离开，起飞，模仿，起程

take office 就职，上任

take one's temperature 量体温

take place 发生，举行

take pride in 以……为荣，对……骄傲

take it easy 别着急，慢慢来

take one's place 就座，入座

take part in 参与，参加

take the place of 代替

（11）以turn为中心：

in one's turn 轮到某人做某事

take one's turn to do 轮到某人做

turn against 背叛，采取敌对态度

turn down 关小，调低，驳回，拒绝

turn to...for help 求助于

turn on 打开；依靠，取决于

turn out 培养，证明是

turn over a new leaf 重新开始，改过自新

turn（a）round 旋转，转过身来

turn upside down 颠倒过来，使陷入混乱

out of turn 不按次序的，不合时宜的

turn a blind eye to 对……视而不见

turn back 折回，往回走

turn into 走进；变成，变为

turn off 关上，辞退，避开（问题）

turn one's attention to 把注意力转向

3. 以介词、副词为中心的常见短语

（1）动词+about：

speak / talk about 谈论

care about 关心，在乎

set about 着手，开始

hear about 听说

think about 思考

bring about 引起，使发生

come about 发生

worry about 为……担心

（2）动词+away：

throw away 扔掉

carry away 拿走

die away 逐渐消失，减弱

wash away 冲走

put away 收拾，储蓄

wear away 磨损，消耗

send away 让走开

blow away 吹走

clear away 清除

pass away 去世

take away 拿走，使消失

give away 泄露，赠送

break away 摆脱

turn away 把……打发走

（3）动词+back：

keep back 隐瞒

look back（on）回顾

hold back 控制住

give back 归还

call back 回电话

take back 拿回，收回

（4）动词+for：

run for 竞选

ask for 要求得到

wait for 等候

stand for 代表，表示

long for 渴望

hope / wish for 希望得到

care for 照顾，关心，喜欢

beg for 乞求

search for 查找

look for 寻找

call for 需要，要求

hunt for 寻找

change...for 用……换

charge...for 收费，要价

apply for 申请

take...for 误以为……是

seek for 寻找

come for 来拿，来取

（5）动词+down：

burn down 烧毁

break down 坏（垮）了，分解

take down 记下，记录

turn down 调小，拒绝

cut down 削减，砍倒

slow down 慢下来

pass down 传下来

put down 记下，镇压

calm down 平静下来

bring down 使……降低

settle down 安家

come down 下落，传下

tear down 拆毁，拆除

（6）动词+at：

come at 袭击

shout at 冲（某人）嚷嚷

run at 冲向，向……攻击

work at 从事

tear at 用力撕

look at 看，注视

stare at 凝视

glare at 怒视

glance at 匆匆一瞥

laugh at 嘲笑

knock at 敲（门、窗等）

point at 指向

smile at 冲……笑

strike at 向……打击

aim at 向……瞄准

shoot at 向……射击

wonder at 惊讶

call at 拜访（某地）

（7）动词+from：

differ from 与……不同

suffer from 受……苦

hear from 收到……来信

die from 因……而死

keep...from 阻止做某事

stop...from 阻止做某事

prevent...from 阻止做某事

learn from 向……学习

result from 由……引起

date from 追溯到

separate...from 把……分开

（8）动词+of：

think of 想到

dream of 梦到

consist of 由……组成

speak of 谈到

approve of 赞成

die of 死于

talk of 谈到

complain of 抱怨

hear of 听说

become of 发生……情况

（9）动词+off：

start off 出发

set off 出发，引爆

leave off 中断

show off 炫耀

get off 下车

take off 脱下，起飞，成功

see off 送行

ring off 挂断电话

put off 延期，推迟

come off 脱落，褪色

cut off 切断，断绝

fall off 跌落，掉下

keep off 避开，勿走近

go off 爆炸；（电）中断；对……失去兴趣

knock...off 把……撞落

break off 打断

pay off 还清

carry off 带走，赢得

give off 散发出

turn（switch）off 关掉

（10）动词+on：

depend on 依靠

rely on 依靠

insist on 坚持

keep on 继续

put on 穿上，戴上，上演

turn（switch）on 打开

live on 以……为生

feed on 以……为食

take on 雇用，呈现（新面貌等）

have on 穿着

look on 旁观

carry on 继续，进行

spend...on 在……花钱

go on 继续

call on 拜访

move on 继续移动，往前走

bring on 使……发展

try on 试穿

pass on 传授，传递

（11）动词+out：

break out 爆发

pick out 选出

burst out 迸发

carry out 执行，进行

hold out 坚持下去

wear out 穿破，使……疲劳

make out 理解，看清楚

cross out 划掉

keep out of 使不进入，挡住

find out 查出，弄明白

try out 试用，试验

put out 扑灭

hand out 散发

run out 用完

let out 泄露，发出，出租

point out 指出

figure out 算出，理解

bring out 生产；出版，使表现出

help out 救助

set out 出发，着手，摆放

turn out 结果是，生产，培养

come out 出版，出来

leave out 省略，删掉

work out 算出，想出办法

give out 散发，分发，用完

look out 当心，提防

speak out 大胆讲出

send out 发出，派遣

die out 灭绝

go out 熄灭

（12）动词+in：

give in 让步

bring in 引进，赚得

result in 导致

join in 参加

hand in 上交

drop in 顺便拜访

succeed in 在……获成功

take in 接纳，吸收，理解

get in 收获，进入

call in 召集，来访

persist in 坚持

（13）动词+into：

look into 研究，调查

burst into 突然爆发

change...into 把……变成

run into 碰到

（14）动词+over：

turn over 翻转，细想

go over 仔细检查，仔细研究

get over 克服

take over 接管，接替

fall over 跌倒，摔倒

（15）动词+to：

belong to 属于

refer to 谈到，涉及，参阅

turn to 向……求助，查阅

see to 处理，料理

reply to 答复

bring to 使苏醒

agree to 同意

supply...to 向……提供

add to 增添

devote...to 致力于

（16）动词+up：

grow up 成长，长大

build up 建立

put up 搭起，住宿，张贴

go up 增长，上涨

break in 强制进入，插话

cut in 插入

fill in 填写

turn into 变成

divide...into 把……分成

translate...into 把……译成

send sb to / into 使某人进入某种状态

think over 仔细考虑

look over 翻阅，检查

run over 碾过，看一遍

watch over 看守，照看

roll over 翻滚

object to 反对

point to 指向

stick / hold / keep to 坚持

come to 共计，苏醒

get to 到达

compare...to 把……比作

write to 写信给

lead to 导致，通向

attend to 处理，专心，照料

tend to 倾向，偏重

give up 放弃，献出

set up 架起，建立

do up 整理，包装，打扮

get up 起床，站起

pick up 拾起，学会，接　　　　bring up 抚养，呕吐，提出

turn up 开大，出现　　　　　　stay up 挺住，熬夜

take up 从事，占据　　　　　　sit up 坐直，熬夜

eat up 吃完　　　　　　　　　use up 用完

tear up 撕碎　　　　　　　　　lay up 卧床歇工

make up 构成，编造，弥补　　　cut up 切碎

join up 联合起来，参军　　　　end up 以……结束

come up 上来，长出，出现　　　speed up 加快速度

throw up 呕吐　　　　　　　　clear up 整理，收拾，放晴

look up 查找，找出　　　　　　burn up 烧毁

catch up 赶上　　　　　　　　hurry up 赶快

fix up 修理，安排，装置　　　　keep up 保持

hold up 耽搁，举起，阻碍　　　send up 发射

ring up 打电话　　　　　　　　open up 打开，开发，开放

break up 分解，破裂，撕毁合同

（17）动词+through：

get through 通过，干完，接通　　look through 翻阅，仔细查看

go through 审阅，通过　　　　　put...through 接通电话

break through 突破　　　　　　see through 识破

pull through 渡过危机，康复

（18）动词+with：

deal with 处理，对付　　　　　do with 处理，需要

meet with 遇到，遭受　　　　　talk with 同……交谈

agree with 同意，与……一致　　compare with 与……相比

combine with 与……相联合　　equip...with 以……装备

cover...with 用……覆盖　　　　begin with 以……开始

end up with 以……结束　　　　supply...with 向……提供

provide...with 向……提供　　　play with 玩，玩弄

Exercise Seven

（一）单句语法填空

1. The computer system broke_____suddenly while he was searching for information on the Internet.

2. Why do we have to put up_____Susan's selfish behavior? We have to teach her to care for others.

3. My mother told me not_____（spend）too much time on the Internet.

4. I make it as a basic rule that I must finish my homework before _____（watch）TV every day.

5. Last night I got a headache, so I took the medicine, but it_____no difference.

6. My mother opened the drawer to put_____the knives and spoons so that we could use them next time.

7. With the test to come, she couldn't go to sleep easily. Thoughts crowded _____and images flashed into her mind.

8.—Sorry, I have to hang_____now. It's time for class.

—OK, I'll call back later.

9. Repeated purchases accounted_____73% of all our sales.

10. After many efforts he finally_____professor in this university in 2018.

（二）单句改错

1. What does this meal spend $ 150?

2. Don't be taken out by products promising to make you lose weight quickly.

3. "Goodbye, then." she said, without even look up from her book.

4. American Indians make up of about five percent of the U.S. population.

5. He told me that he would lend me his book after he finished read the last part.

6. He telephoned the travel agency to booked three air tickets to London.

7. Practicing kung fu can not only build one's strength, but also develop one's character.

8. We have just moved into a bigger house and there's a lot to do. Let's get down on it.

9. The new movie promises to one of the biggest money-makers of all time.

10. Doing morning exercise will do good for your health.

（三）语法填空

阅读下面材料，在空白处填入适当的内容（1个单词）或括号内单词的正确形式。

I always dreamed of ___1___ (travel) on my own. But my parents worried ___2___ me all the time. They thought I might have trouble ___3___ solving the problems I came ___4___. In order to comfort them, I decided ___5___ travel with a friend and they agreed. It ___6___ (take) me just two minutes to book two train tickets from my hometown to Nanjing, paying with Alipay. I also downloaded an App which ___7___ (use) to help me find the hotel easily. We spent several days ___8___ (visit) Nanjing's great places ___9___ (include) many old museums, which contained a number of beautiful paintings. Although this was the first time that I ___10___ (leave) home, I really had a good time.

（四）短文改错

On the hot afternoon of last Saturday, Li Yue went downtown and walked from one store to another, looking after the clothes we would wear in the singing contest. While the rest of us was enjoying our time in cool and comfortable rooms, she spent the whole afternoon searching and select. Finally she found out the suitable clothes. Deeply move by what she did, we tried our better and won the first prize in the contest. Li Yue always care for the class. She often devotes her spare time to help others. She has set a good example for us. Therefore, she deserves the honor and we should learn of her.

第八章　动词的时态和语态

英语的动词时态是学习重点，是学好英语需要掌握的内容之一，也是学生学习语法时的一大难点，尤其是一般过去时、现在完成时、过去进行时之间的区别。英语中的动词时态按照时间可分为现在、过去、将来和过去将来，按照动作可分为一般、进行、完成及完成进行，因此共有十六种时态，见下表（以动词do为例）：

时间 动作	现在	过去	将来	过去将来
一般	do / does	did	will do	would do
进行	am / is / are doing	was / were doing	will be doing	would be doing
完成	have / has done	had done	will have done	would have done
完成进行	have / has been doing	had been doing	will have been doing	would have been doing

一、常见动词时态的用法

1. 一般现在时

（1）表示现在经常性或者习惯性的动作或存在的状态，通常与一般现在时连用的时间状语有：always, usually, often, frequently, sometimes, seldom, every day, once a week, now and then, at times, occasionally。例如：

He **gets** up early and **goes** to bed early every day.

他每天早起早睡。

She **is** our English teacher and she **is** very kind to her students.

她是我们的英语老师，她对学生们很和蔼。

（2）表示客观事实或者普遍真理，由直接引语变为间接引语时，时态不变，仍然用一般现在时。例如：

The sun **rises** in the east and **sets** in the west.

太阳从东方升起，西方落下。

He told his students that light **travels** faster than sound.

他告诉他的学生光比声音传播速度快。

（3）在时刻表中可以表示按计划将要发生的动作，常用动词有：come，go，leave，start，stay，return，arrive，begin，end，take，have等。例如：

The train **leaves** at 8 a.m. and **arrives** at Beijing at 6 p.m. tomorrow.

这趟火车上午8点出发，明天下午6点到达北京。

The third class **begins** at 10：10 and **ends** at 10：55.

第三节课10：10开始，10：55结束。

（4）当主句为将来时态的时候，在when，while，if，unless，as soon as等引导的状语从句中代替将来时，即所谓的"主将从现"。例如：

I will go to visit the museum with my teacher **if** he is free tomorrow afternoon.

如果老师明天下午有时间的话，我将和他一起去参观博物馆。

She will buy me some stamps **while** she is in the post office this afternoon.

她今天下午在邮局时，会给我买几张邮票。

2. 一般过去时

（1）表示动作在过去某个时候发生或完成，也表示过去存在的状态，跟现在没有联系。经常与一般过去时连用的时间状语有：yesterday，the other day，last month，five years ago，in 1999，then等。例如：

He **went** to Nanjing in 2000 and **came** back last month.

2000年他去南京，上个月回来了。

The other day I **met** your mother in the street and she was in black.

前几天我在街上碰见你妈妈，她当时穿着一身黑衣服。

（2）表示过去经常发生的动作，常跟used to，usually，always，frequently，often连用。例如：

My grandfather **used** to tell us stories when we **were** little children.

我们小的时候爷爷经常给我们讲故事。

（3）表示某一动作在过去持续了一段时间后终止或发生了若干次。例如：

My father **worked** in the shoe factory for 10 years.

我爸爸在那家鞋厂里工作过十年。

He **went** to Shanghai for business meetings three times last year.

去年他三次去上海开商务会议。

3. 一般将来时

表示将要发生的动作或存在的状态叫作一般将来时，常跟tomorrow, in the future, from now on, next year, in three hours等时间状语连用。通常有以下五种方式：

（1）will, shall表示单纯客观的将来，多用于书面语中，比较正式。例如：

He **will be** eighteen years old next month and we are going to hold a ceremony to celebrate it.

他下个月就十八岁了，我们打算举行仪式庆祝一下。

The president **will attend** the summit and visit four countries soon.

总统即将出席峰会并访问四国。

（2）be going to表示打算做某事，多用于口语中，也可表示天气预测。例如：

I **am going to** take my parents around the world if I have enough time and money.

如果我有足够的时间和钱的话，我打算带父母周游世界。

Look at the clouds in the sky, it **is going to** rain soon.

看看天上的云，马上要下雨。

（3）be to do表示安排、计划好的事情要发生或者"应该"做某事。例如：

She **is to go** to America for further education next month according to the schedule.

根据计划她将于下个月去美国深造。

You **are to report** it to the teacher if the same thing happens again.

如果类似的事情再次发生，你们应该向老师汇报。

（4）be about to do表示即将发生的动作，但不能与表示将来时间的状语连用。例如：

They **are about to finish** their homework and we **are about to go** to the cinema together.

他们马上就做完作业了，然后我们就一起去看电影。

They **are about to finish** their homework in five minutes. （此句错误，因为不能与时间状语连用）

（5）come，go，leave，stay，return，start，take，have等动词的一般现在时和现在进行时也可表示即将发生的动作或预定的动作，一般现在时多用于时刻表中。例如：

Dear passengers，please fasten your safe belts. The plane **is taking off** soon.

亲爱的旅客朋友，请系好安全带，飞机马上就要起飞了。

The train Z56 **starts** from Lanzhou at 21：11 and **arrives** at Beijing at 13：38 the next day.

Z56次列车21：11从兰州出发，次日13：38到达北京。

4. 现在完成时

（1）表示过去发生或者已经完成的动作对现在造成的影响或结果，经常与already，yet，so far，recently，lately，up to now，never，ever，this year等连用。例如：

I **have already seen** the film. It's so interesting and exciting.

我已经看过那部电影了，它既有趣又令人兴奋。

I **have already had** my lunch，so I am not hungry at all.

我已经吃过午饭了，所以一点都不饿。

（2）表示从过去开始，一直延续到现在的动作或状态，有可能延续下去，这种情况下只能用延续性动词，不能用短暂性动词，经常与表示一段时间的状语连用，如for five years，since 1999，in / during / over past（last）few years，all the time等。例如：

We **have lived** here since we came back from America.

我们从美国回来以后一直住在这里。

They **have studied** Japanese in the past five years and much progress **has been made** so far.

他们在过去五年里一直学习日语并且到目前为止已经取得了很大进步。

试翻译：**他已经离开家十年了**。

He has left home for ten years. （错误。因为短暂性动词不能与表示一段时间的状语连用）

He has been away from home for ten years. （正确。用形容词替代短暂性动词）

It is ten years since he left home. （正确）

He left home ten years ago. （正确）

（3）have been和have gone，前者表示"去过某地且已经回来"，后者表示"去了某地还没回来"，有可能到达目的地或在途中。例如：

She **has been** to the United Kingdom of Great Britain and Northern Ireland. （已经回来）

她去过大不列颠及北爱尔兰联合王国。

She **has gone** to the United Kingdom of Great Britain and Northern Ireland. （还没回来）

她去了大不列颠及北爱尔兰联合王国。

（4）常用现在完成时的其他句式有：

It is the first time that I **have experienced** such a terrible earthquake.

这是我第一次经历如此可怕的地震。

This is the most interesting movie that I **have ever seen** in my life.

这是我有生以来看过的最有趣的电影。

The game will have to be put off if the rain **hasn't stopped** by 3 o'clock this afternoon.

如果今天下午3点以前雨不停的话，比赛不得不推迟。（现在完成时代替了将来完成时）

Once you **have made** a promise，you should keep it and never break it.

你一旦许下诺言，就要遵守，不能食言。

5. 现在进行时

（1）表示说话时正在进行而没有完成的动作。例如：

I **am standing and speaking**，you **are sitting and listening** now.

我站着说着，你坐着听着。

（2）表示当前一段时间内正在进行的动作，说话时不一定正在进行。例如：

I **am travelling** and my sister **is writing** a novel these days.

这些日子我在旅游，我姐姐在写一部小说。

People's life **is becoming** better and better with the development of economy.

随着经济的发展，人们的生活变得越来越好。

（3）与always，constantly，frequently连用，表示说话人赞扬或厌恶的感情色彩。例如：

She **is always helping** those who are in need of help.（赞扬）

她总是帮助那些需要帮助的人。

She **is constantly standing** in front of the mirror, making herself up.（厌恶）

她总是站在镜子前面，打扮自己。

（4）come，go，leave，stay，return，start，take，have等动词的现在进行时表示即将发生的动作或预定的动作。例如：

We **are leaving** for Shanghai tomorrow morning.

我们明天早晨动身去上海。

（5）表示感觉、情感、存在、从属、思维等的动词不用于进行时，如：exist，belong to，fear，hate，remember，forget，know，believe，want，need，understand，please，respect，prefer，mind，like，dislike，hope，wish，agree，appreciate，recognize，mean，care，love，accept，allow，admit，refuse，promise，decide，look（看起来），sound（听起来），smell（闻起来），taste（尝起来），feel（摸起来）等。

6. 过去进行时

（1）表示过去某一刻或某一段时间正在进行的动作，常用的时间状语有at that time，at this time yesterday，at that moment以及when，while引导的从句等。例如：

He **was writing** a composition at this time yesterday while she **was reading** the newspaper.

昨天这个时候他在写文章而她在看报纸。

The reporter said that the UFO **was travelling** very fast from east to west when he saw it.

记者说当他看见不明飞行物时它正从东向西飞速驶过。

（2）跟always，constantly，frequently连用，表示说话人赞扬或厌恶的感情色彩。例如：

He **was always cleaning** the blackboard when he was at school.（赞扬）

他上学期间一直擦黑板。

She **was always** throwing things wherever she liked.（厌恶）

她总是把东西随意乱扔。

（3）come，go，leave，stay，return，start，take，have，get等动词的过去进行时表示过去即将发生的动作或预定的动作。例如：

Mr. Smith said that he **was leaving** for London soon.

史密斯先生说他马上动身去伦敦。

7. 过去完成时

（1）表示在过去某一时间或者在某个动作之前已经完成的动作或状态，常用before，until after，by the time，by the end of等引导的时间状语。例如：

We **had learned** ten lessons of New Concept English by the end of last term.

到上学期末为止，我们已经学了十篇新概念英语课文。

When he arrived at the cinema, the film **had already begun** and the lights **had been** out.

当他到电影院时，电影已经开始，灯也已经熄灭。

（2）表示从过去某一时间开始一直延续到过去另一时间为止的动作，只用延续性动词，常用for，since，when，until等引导的时间状语。例如：

I **had taught** English in that junior school for five years before I came to this school.

我在来这所学校之前，在那所初级中学教了五年英语。

They **had known** each other for three years before they got married.

他们认识三年后才结的婚。

（3）表示过去打算但没有实现的愿望或意图，常用的动词有：hope，expect，intend，want，suppose，mean等。例如：

I **had intended** to make a speech at the meeting but nobody would like to give me such a chance.

我本来打算在会上发个言，但没人愿意给我这样一个机会。

I **had supposed** that she got married at least 10 years ago，but she is still single.

我原以为她至少十年前就结婚了，但她仍然是单身。

（4）用于虚拟语气的从句以及某些句式中表示与过去事实相反。例如：

If I **had met** you yesterday，I would have told you the good news.

如果我昨天碰见你的话，我会告诉你那个好消息的。

I wish that I **had passed** the examination last time.

我真希望我上次通过考试了。

If only she **had attended** the meeting yesterday.

她昨天要是去开会就好了。

I would rather he **had chosen** science instead of art.

我宁愿他选择了理科而不是文科。

Hardly（No sooner）**had** he **finished** his homework when（than）he was sent to clean the room.

他刚做完作业就被派去打扫房间。

She asked me whether I **had taken** part in the discussion.

她问我是否参加了那场讨论。

8. 过去将来时

表示从过去看来将要发生的动作或存在的状态，常用下列形式：

（1）would / should +动词原形。例如：

He said that he **would go** to Shanghai to attend the business conference the next week.

他说他下周将去上海出席商业会议。

（2）was / were going to do 表示过去打算或者计划做某事。例如：

I **was going to have** a picnic with my friends，but suddenly I had a more important thing to deal with.

我打算跟朋友去野餐，但突然又有更重要的事要处理。

（3）was / were（about）to do 表示过去计划或安排将要做某事。例如：

He **was just about to give** me the map when someone knocked at the door.

他正要给我地图，这个时候有人敲门了。

（4）was / were doing 表示过去进行时，有时候也表示过去将要发生的动作。例如：

He **was setting** off for Beijing early the next morning.

他第二天一大早就动身去北京。

9. 现在完成进行时

表示从过去开始一直延续到现在，并且还在进行的动作，具有完成和进行双特征，即现在完成时+现在进行时，不能用短暂性动词。例如：

He **has been whitewashing** the walls for five hours. （还在刷）

他粉刷墙有五个小时了。

The water in the ocean **has been increasing** over the past twenty years. （还在涨）

那片海洋里的水过去二十年一直在涨。

10. 过去完成进行时

表示从过去某一时刻开始一直延续到过去另一时刻，并且在那时还在进行，即过去完成时+过去进行时，不能用短暂性动词。例如：

The crazy fans **had been waiting** for three hours and they would wait till the movie star turned up.

那些疯狂的粉丝等了三个小时了，他们还将继续等，直到电影明星出现。

She **had been living** there since she was born and then she would move to her husband's.

她自出生以来一直住在那儿，然后她将搬到她丈夫家。

11. 将来进行时

强调将来某一时刻正在进行的动作。例如：

Don't be worried. I **will be waiting** for you at the station as soon as you get off the train.

别担忧！你一下火车我就在车站等你。

At this time next week we **will be enjoying** ourselves on the seashore.

下周这个时候我们将在海滨玩得很开心。

12. 将来完成时

表示到将来某一时间为止将要完成的动作。例如：

The construction of the stadium **will have been completed** by the end of next year.

体育馆将在明年年底以前竣工。

They **will have finished** their task on time if they would like to work two extra hours every day.

如果他们愿意每天多工作两个小时，他们将按时完成任务。

二、易混时态区别

1. 一般现在时和现在进行时

一般现在时侧重经常和反复发生的动作或存在的状态，而现在进行时强调此时此刻或现阶段正在进行的动作以及即将发生的动作等。例如：

He **is** a senior school student and he **has** an English class every day except Sunday.

他现在是一名高中生，除星期天外，他每天都上英语课。

He **is having** an English class now and his English **is getting** better and better.

他正在上英语课，他的英语越来越好了。

2. 一般过去时和现在完成时

一般过去时和现在完成时所表示的动作都发生在过去，但一般过去时侧重动作发生在过去，与现在没有关系，往往和一些表示过去的时间状语连用，如 last year, five years ago, in 1999, the other day, just now 等；现在完成时表示发生在过去的动作对现在造成的影响或产生的结果。例如：

—**Have** you **seen** the film?

你看过那部电影了吗？

—Yes, I **have**.（已知道内容）

是的，看过了。

—When and where **did** you see it?

你什么时候在哪里看的？

—I **saw** it in Lanzhou Great Theatre last Wednesday.（侧重动作发生在过去）

上周三在兰州大剧院看的。

—Did you go to London last year? （侧重动作发生在过去）

你去年去伦敦了吗?

—Yes，I did. I have been there twice.（后一句表示对现在造成的影响）

是的。我去过伦敦两次了。

3. 一般过去时和过去进行时

一般过去时表示动作在过去发生且完成，而过去进行时则强调动作在过去某一时刻进行着，有没有结果还不知道。例如：

I wrote a letter this morning.（信已写完）

我今早写了封信。

I was writing a letter this morning.（不知道结果，只侧重"在写"）

我今早在写信。

I slipped into the yard when the guard was looking into the sky.

当门卫看天的那一瞬间我溜进了院子。

4. 一般过去时和过去完成时

一般过去时表示就现在而言的过去发生的动作，而过去完成时强调就过去而言的过去发生或者完成的动作，过去完成时一般都有一个过去时间或者动作作为映衬。例如：

They went to America five days ago.

他们五天前去美国了。

She had already left her home when we arrived there.

当我们到那儿时，她已经离开家了。

5. 现在完成时和现在完成进行时

现在完成时表示发生在过去的动作对现在造成的影响，强调动作已完成，与表示一段时间的状语连用时多表示"长期性"；而现在完成进行时表示某动作从过去开始延续到现在，动作还没有完成，有可能继续下去，往往具有未完结性、短暂性、刚完结性以及连续性等。例如：

I have read *The Story of the Stone* twice.（已完成）

我读过《红楼梦》两遍了。

I have been reading *The Story of the Stone* for a month.（未完结性）

我读《红楼梦》一个月了。

I **have lived** here for 20 years. （长期性）

我在这儿住了20年了。

I **have been living** here for 20 days. （短暂性）

我在这儿住了20天了。

My hands are dirty. I've **been painting** the car. （刚完结性）

我的手很脏，我在给汽车刷油漆来着。

She **has been playing** tennis since she was eight. （连续性）

她自八岁以来一直不断地打网球。

三、被动语态

英语中有主动语态和被动语态两种语态。当句子主语是动作的执行者时，谓语动词就用主动语态；当句子主语是动作的承受者时，就用被动语态，不及物动词没有被动语态。在英语中，被动语态用得比在汉语中多一些。

1. 常用被动语态的情况

（1）当不知道动作的执行者或者没必要说出动作的执行者是谁时。例如：

English is widely used all over the world.

英语在全世界用得很广泛。

Tea was introduced into the United Kingdom from China.

茶是从中国引入英国的。

（2）当强调动作的承受者时。例如：

Health is valued above everything.

健康高于一切。

The book has been translated into many languages.

这本书被翻译成了多种语言。

（3）当动作的承受者是无生命的事物时。例如：

The window was broken this morning by a flying stone.

这个窗户是今早被一块飞石打破的。

2. 被动语态的构成

助动词be +及物动词的过去分词。我们可以通过例句来看常用时态的被动语态。例如：

Breakfast **is served** between 7：00 and 9：00 every morning.

每天上午7：00—9：00供应早餐。

English **was taught** in our school five years ago.

五年前我们学校开设英语。

A business meeting **will be held** in Shanghai next month.

下个月在上海将要召开一个商业大会。

The injured **have been sent** to the nearest hospital.

伤者已经被送到最近的医院。

My car **is being repaired** now，so I have to take a taxi to work.

我的车子正在被修理，因此我不得不打车去上班。

The horse **was being tied** to the tree when I passed by.

我路过时那匹马正被拴在树上。

The construction **had been completed** before I came into power.

在我当权之前建设工作已经完成。

He told his students that all the lessons **would be finished** in a week.

他告诉他的学生说，所有的课一周内将要结束。

3. 被动语态注意事项

（1）含有双宾语的被动语态，可以将任何一个宾语变为被动语态的主语。例如：

有人给了她一些漂亮的花。Someone gave her some beautiful flowers. 可变成：

She was given some beautiful flowers.

Some beautiful flowers were given to her.

（2）短语动词变为被动语态时，任何一个介词或副词都不能省略。例如：

Although she **was** often **made fun of**，she **was taken good care of** there.

尽管她在那儿经常被捉弄，但被照顾得很好。

（3）notice，let，make，hear，listen to，see，look at，watch，observe，have，feel等动词或短语后作宾语补足语的动词不定式要省略to，但变为被动语态时作主语补足语时要加上to。例如：

The boss made the employees **work** as many as 12 hours a day.（主动语态）

The employees were made **to** work as mang as 12 hours a day. （被动语态）

老板让员工每天工作长达12个小时。

Some students were noticed **to enter** the laboratory without permission.

有人注意到一些学生未经允许就进了实验室。

（4）系动词不用被动语态，或者说用主动表被动。例如：

His forehead **feels** hot and he **looks** tired, so he may have a cold.

他的额头摸起来烫，他看起来也有点累，因此，他也许感冒了。

The dish **smells** nice and **tastes** delicious, too.

这道菜闻起来很香，尝起来也很好吃。

（5）有些及物动词表示"……起来"时，常用作不及物动词，没有被动语态，这类动词常见的有：sell, wash, read, write, open, close, measure, weigh等。例如：

This kind of cloth **washes** easily and therefore it **sells** well.

这种布料洗起来容易，所以很畅销。

The case **measures** 60 centimetres long and **weighs** heavily.

这个箱子长60厘米，重得很。

（6）有些及物动词和短语不用于被动式，常见的动词和短语有：begin, finish, start, open, close, fit, have, wish, cost, agree with, suffer from, take part in, walk into, belong to, happen to等。例如：

The shop **opens** at 6:00 a.m. and **closes** at 9:00 p.m..

这个商店早晨6:00开门，晚上9:00关门。

The meeting **began** on May 5th and **finished** on May 9th.

会议于5月5日开幕，5月9日闭幕。

We have many dictionaries and each **cost** us a certain amount of money.

我们有很多字典，每本都花费了我们一定数额的钱。

（7）be to blame主动形式表示被动。例如：

Who **are to blame** for the broken windows?

谁应该为打破的窗户受到责备?

Exercise Eight

（一）单句语法填空

1. We felt rather tired when we got home, so we_____（go）straight to bed.

2. I thought it difficult to follow the lecture because it_____（begin）when I got there.

3. We went to the library to do some reading, only to be told that it _____（decorate）.

4. It is_____（say）that *Jurassic Park* is a very nice film.

5. In the past decades, China_____（make）great achievements in science and technology.

6. —Where is Anna? I can't find her anywhere.

—She went to the library after lunch and_____（write）her essay there ever since.

7. Shakespeare's play *Hamlet*_____（make）into at least ten different films over the past years.

8. If you close the door of fear behind you, you_____（see）the door of faith open before you.

9. There is no doubt that the environment_____（improve）by our further efforts to reduce pollution.

10. The number of deaths from lung cancer will reduce greatly if more people_____（persuade）to give up smoking.

（二）单句改错

1. English is speaking all over the world.

2. It is the third time that I had seen the film.

3. We have hardly left home when it began to rain hard.

4. We saw a girl crying in the rain and inviting her to take shelter from the rain in our coffee shop.

5. Last week my parents went to Norway on tour. I left alone, with no one talking to me.

6. The couple adopted the baby when she was only several days old and can't even open her eyes.

7. By the time you will arrive in Britain, we'll have stayed there for three weeks.

8. As she knows, I have been made some new friends here these years.

9. They promised they will not tell the press our plan the day before yesterday.

10. The water supply has been cut off temporarily because some workers are repaired the main pipe.

（三）语法填空

阅读下面材料，在空白处填入适当的内容（1个单词）或括号内单词的正确形式。

My best friend Amy is sitting alone in the classroom, which____1____（remind）me of myself. In the past, I____2____（be）never confident because of my disability. People always laughed at me. At that time I was unable to run and play like other children and I gradually started getting depressed. However, someone told me something that I will always remember.

It was in one October. Surrounded by a group of girls who____3____（point）at me and laughed at me, I couldn't help crying. The tears rolled down my face like a rushing river. To my surprise, someone lifted my head up and wiped the tears from my eyes.

I then knew it was our English teacher, Miss Wang. She said, "You____4____（be）perfect the way you are. You should never change or hate yourself. People____5____（accept）you for who you____6____（be）. But if you cannot accept yourself, then how will other people accept you?" I____7____（inspire）by her words. Over the past few months, I____8____（learn）that no one is perfect and that we all have flaws. Now I have wonderful friends who____9____（love）me for who I am.

Now, seeing Amy cry, I decide to tell her the same thing Miss Wang ____10____（tell）me.

（四）短文改错

Last month our class held a great activity which required us form a good habit in 30 days. I gladly paired up with Greece, my deskmate. First, we discussed what habit we will develop. All of us agreed to read for half an hour every day. Then we made a list of the books we were interesting in. From then on, we managed to spare half an hour every day to read books, however busy we are. Besides, we took a lot of notes and often exchange ideas. In the end, we had accomplished our goal of read for 30 days. How proud we were! More importantly, I had kept on reading every day since then and reading books have become an essential part of my life.

第九章　情态动词

情态动词常用来表达说话人的情感态度，对某一事物的看法、倾向、好恶程度等，也表达请求、命令、警告、赞扬、厌恶等情感。

一、情态动词的基本用法

（1）表示征求意见或许可的情态动词有must，can，may，might，shall等。例如：

—Must I hand in my composition today?

我今天必须交作文吗？

—Yes，you must.

是的，必须交。

—Must I hand in my composition today?

我今天必须交作文吗？

—No，you needn't.（否定回答时可用needn't）

不，没必要。

Can he ask for a leave tomorrow and the day after tomorrow?

他明天和后天可以请个假吗？

May / Might I sit in the front of the bus?　（用might语气更委婉）

我可以坐在公共汽车前部吗？

Shall I open the window to let in some fresh air?　（shall此用法只用于第一人称和第三人称）

我可以打开窗户放进一些新鲜空气吗？

Shall he come to see you now that he is your relative?

既然他是你的亲戚，那他可以进来见你吗？

（2）表示邀请或请求的情态动词有can，will，would，could，用于第二人称，用would 和could 时表示语气更加委婉。例如：

Can / Could you give me some advice on how to learn English grammar?

你能给我一些如何学习英语语法的建议吗？

Will / Would you please tell me where the nearest hospital is?

请告诉我最近的医院在哪里，好吗？

（3）表示允许或许可的情态动词有can，may。例如：

You **can** sit where I used to sit，it's very comfortable.

你可以坐在我过去常坐的地方，很舒服的。

You **may** stay at home for a few days instead of going to work.

你可以在家里待几天而不用去上班。

（4）表示禁止的情态动词有can't，mustn't，shan't等否定形式。例如：

They **can't** wear whatever they like when they are at school.

他们在学校不能想穿什么就穿什么。

Anybody **mustn't** take books out of the reading room.

任何人都不能把书带出阅览室。

You **shan't** make any noise as soon as you are in the reading room.

一进入阅览室你就不能吵闹了。

（5）表示建议或劝告的情态动词有ought to，should，had better，need等。例如：

You **ought to** take good care of your parents when they are old. （ought to表示义务）

父母年迈时，你应该照顾好他们。

You **should** do proper amounts of exercise to improve your health.

你应该适度锻炼以促进身体健康。

You **had better** put on more clothes in case it is cold on the mountain.

你最好多穿点衣服，以防山上冷。

In order to learn English well，you **need** practice speaking English more often.

为了学好英语，你需要更经常地练习说英语。

（6）表示能力的情态动词有 can，could，be able to等。can 表示现在的"能力"，could表示过去的"能力"，be able to 用来填充can，could没有的时态，但 was / were able to 表示"过去设法做成功某事"，等于managed to do something或 succeeded in doing something，此用法不能被could 代替。例如：

When I was at school I **couldn't** speak English，but now I can speak it rather fluently.

上学的时候我不会讲英语，但现在我讲得相当流利。

I am sure he will **be able to** support his family in the future.

我确信他将来能够养活他的家庭。

They charged 20 thousand dollars for the car but I **was able to** bring the price down.

那辆车他们要价两万美元，但我设法把价格压了下来。

（7）表示推测的情态动词有 must，may，might，can，could，should，ought to等。must 表推测语气最强，但只用于肯定式，否定式中用can't或 couldn't代替；must / may / might / can't / could / couldn't + have done表示对过去发生事情的推测；should，ought to 表示"按理说应该"。例如：

It **may** be the headmaster's office，I am not sure.

这也许是校长办公室，我不太确定。

He was careless. He **might** have won the first place otherwise.

他粗心了，否则他也许会赢得第一名。

—Who **can** it be?

那个人可能是谁?

—It **must** be our headmaster.

一定是我们校长。

—No，it **can't** be him. He is in America now.

不可能是他，他现在在美国。

—Was it in the classroom that he smoked yesterday?

昨天他是在教室吸烟的吗?

—It **could** be in the office，but I am not sure.

有可能在办公室，但我不确定。

There were five people in your car during the long journey. It **must** have been uncomfortable.

漫长的旅途中你车子上坐了五个人，那一定不舒服。

He was with me at the meeting yesterday. He **couldn't have** played computer games in the net bar.

他昨天跟我在一起开会，他一定没有在网吧玩电脑游戏。

He **should** be over fifteen years old，because he is a student in Senior Two.

按理说他应该超过十五岁了，因为他已经是高二的学生了。

She **ought to** turn up at any moment，for she is never late for work.

按理说她随时就会到达，因为她上班从来不迟到。

（8）表示轻微埋怨、责备或后悔时，用情态动词should / ought to / needn't / could / might + have done来表示。例如：

The flower has died. You **should / ought to** have given it more water.（表示过去应该做而没做）

这盆花死了。你应该给它多浇点水。

I have a stomachache. I **shouldn't / oughtn't** to have eaten so much fried chicken.（表示过去不应该做而做了）

我胃疼。我不应该吃那么多的炸鸡。

I **needn't** have lent her so much money. She had more money than she needed actually.（表示过去做了没必要做的事情）

我没必要借给她那么多钱。事实上，她有更多的闲钱。

Don't throw bottles out of the window any more. You **could** have hurt anyone passing by.（表示过去完全有可能发生但没发生的动作）

不要再向窗外扔瓶子了，你会伤到过路人的。

She was out of mind. She **might** have done it much better otherwise.（表示过去有可能做但没做）

她当时心不在焉，否则她会做得好得多。

（9）表示警告、允诺、命令或威胁的情态动词是shall，常用于第二、三人称。例如：

You **shall** have whatever you like as your birthday present，as long as you do well in the exams.

只要你考试考得好，我允诺你的生日礼物可以是任何你喜欢的东西。

All the candidates **shall** remain at their seats until the bell rings announcing the end of the exam.

所有考生都必须待在座位上，直到宣布考试结束的铃声响。

（10）表示偏执的情态动词是must。例如：

If you **must** want to know my age，let me tell you unwillingly.

如果你非要知道我的年龄，我就勉强告诉你吧。

Must you play the piano at such a late hour?

你非要在深夜弹奏钢琴吗?

（11）表示怀疑的情态动词有should（竟然），dare，can't。例如：

Such an educated gentleman **should** be so rude to that girl.

这么有文化的一位绅士竟然对那个女孩如此粗鲁。

How **dare** you say that I treated you unfairly?

你怎么敢说我对你不公平?

Why **can't** you know my telephone number and e-mail address?

你怎么会不知道我的电话和邮件地址呢?

（12）表示习惯性的情态动词有will，would，will表示现在反复，would表示过去反复。例如：

Every day after work he **will** go to the cafe to have a cup of coffee.

每天下班之后他都去那个咖啡馆喝杯咖啡。

Every time he is in trouble，he **will** come to me for help.

每次他处于麻烦之中的时候，他都会来找我帮忙。

He **would** cross the border frequently in those days，driving a bicycle with an empty straw bag.

那些日子他频繁地越过边界线，推着一辆自行车，上面放着一个空空的草袋子。

Whenever and wherever he met him，he **would** stop the soldier and ask the same questions again and again in those days.

在那些日子里，无论何时何地他碰见那个士兵都会拦住，一遍遍地问相同的问题。

二、情态动词用法区别及其他

1. must & have to

must表示主观上"必须"；have to表示客观逼迫，"不得不"。例如：

We **must** get up early and do morning exercises，which I like very much.

我们必须早早起来做早操，这是我非常喜欢的。

I don't like to get up early on Sunday，but I **have to**，because I have a lot of things to do.

星期天我不喜欢早起，但我不得不起来，因为有很多事情要做。

2. could & was / were able to

could表示过去的"能力"，可以被was / were able to替换，而was / were able to表示"过去一次性设法做成……"，相当于managed to do sth.，或succeeded in doing sth.，此用法不能被could代替。

I **could** swim when I was seven years old.

我七岁时就会游泳。

A terrible earthquake happened suddenly but all of us **were able to** get out of the classroom.

一场可怕的地震突然发生，但是我们都设法从教室里逃了出来。

3. would，used to，be used to doing & be used to do sth.

would表示过去反复的动作，而used to则侧重"过去如此，现在已经不是那样了"以及"过去存在的状态"；be used to doing表示"习惯于做某事"，其中be有时态和人称的变化，to后跟动名词；be used to do sth. 表示"某东西被用来做某事"。例如：

When he was in that company he **would** go to that coffee shop at the corner after work every day.

当他在那家公司上班的时候，每天下班后都去拐角处的咖啡屋。

He **used to** smoke and drink a lot.（表示现在已经不是那样了）

他过去吸烟酗酒。

There **used to** be a big tree where our classroom was.（过去的状态）

过去我们教室所在的地方有一棵大树。

He has **been used to** working in such bad conditions.

他已经习惯于在如此恶劣的条件下工作。

Wood can **be used to** make desks and beds and so on.

木头可以用来制成桌子和床等。

4. didn't need to do & needn't have done

didn't need to do表示"过去没必要做也没做"，而needn't have done表示"过去没必要做但已经做了"。例如：

It was raining yesterday. I **didn't need to** work in the fields，so I stayed at home.

昨天下着雨，我没必要去地里干活，所以我在家里待着。

It was Sunday yesterday. I **needn't have gone** to school. But I forgot it and went as usual.

昨天是星期天，我没必要去上学，但是我忘了，所以和往常一样去了。

5. need & dare

这两个词既可用作情态动词，也可用作实义动词。一般来说，作情态动词时多用于否定句和疑问句；作实义动词时用于各种句式，后跟动词不定式，I dare say是固定短语，意为"我认为、我相信"。例如：

—**Need** I finish my report by six o'clock today?

我今天六点以前需要写完报告吗？

—Yes，you must / you have to. / No，you **needn't** / you don't have to.

是的，你必须要写完。/ 不，没必要。

As a senior high school student，I **need** to work at least 10 hours a day.

作为一名高中生，我需要每天学习至少10个小时。

My car **needs** repairing / to be repaired thoroughly.（动名词主动表被动）

我的车子需要彻底修理。

Tom **daren't** go out alone when it is dark at night.

汤姆晚上天黑时不敢一人出去。

Dare you go home to face your parents when you haven't done well in the exams?

你考试没考好时敢回家面对父母吗？

I don't **dare** to feel the snake even if it is dead.

即使那条蛇死了，我也不敢去摸。

6. should & ought to

should表示"命令，劝告"等意，而ought to表示"有义务、责任"，语气比should强，但比must弱。例如：

You **should** keep quiet when others are answering the teacher's questions.

当别人回答老师问题的时候，你应该保持安静。

We **ought to** take good care of our parents when they are old.

当父母年迈的时候，我们有义务好好照顾他们。

7. can't have done & couldn't have done / could have done

can't have done和couldn't have done均可表示must的否定推测，强调从现在角度出发推测过去某事"不可能"。但当主句的谓语动词是过去式时，就必须用couldn't have done。could have done表示"过去有能力或有可能做某事但没有做"，有惋惜、遗憾、批评、责备等意思。例如：

His schoolbag is here，so he **can't**（**couldn't**）have gone home.

他的书包还在这儿，因此他不可能回家去。

My sister met him at the Grand Theatre yesterday，so he **couldn't** have attended your lecture.

我姐姐昨天在大剧院碰见他了，所以他不可能去听你的讲座。

You **could** have walked here instead of taking a taxi. It is so near.

你完全可以走到这里，不用打车的。距离很近。

8. would like to do & would like to have done

would like to do 表示现在或将来"想做某事"，而would like to have done表示过去"想做某事但没做成"。例如：

I **would like to** go to the concert tonight，but my parents don't allow me to.

我今晚想去听音乐会，但我爸妈不让。

I **would like to** have gone to the concert last night but I had to review lessons for the exams.

我昨晚想去听音乐会的，但我不得不为考试而复习功课。

Exercise Nine

（一）单句语法填空

1. —How's your tour to Lake Baikal? Is it really beautiful?

   —It_____be, but it is now polluted.

2. Who _____ it be that left the window open?

3. —Will you tell me your secret?

   —Sorry, I _____. It wouldn't be a secret if I told you.

4. _____ you please help us send the injured to the hospital?

5. I believe that a journalist _____ be completely objective.

6. —What are you going to do this weekend?

   —I don't know. I _____ go to the Summer Palace.

7. —Some people are really curious about what their neighbors are doing.

   —Curiosity sometimes _____ be foolish or wrong.

8. I've ordered some takeout, so we_____worry about cooking when we get home tired.

9. Since nobody lent him a hand, he_____have done the research on his own.

10. —Sorry, Mum! I failed the test again.

    —Oh, it's too bad. You_____have made full preparations.

（二）单句改错

1. You shouldn't be too careful when you are driving in the street!

2. It is so noisy here that I mustn't hear what you are saying.

3. You might be John. You haven't changed a bit after all these years.

4. Although you need find bargains here, it's not generally a cheap place to shop.

5. I can still remember those happy days when my parents will take me to Disneyland at weekends.

6. "Nobody will carry a mobile phone into the examination room during the

national college entrance examinations," the head teacher said.

7. Only by working hard to pursue our dreams we enjoy a meaningful and fulfilled life.

8. Each time she was in trouble, she went to Grandpa for help, as he said he might do anything to help her.

9. He mustn't have gone too far. His coffee is still warm.

10. Mr. Green shouldn't have been at yesterday's party because he had left the day before yesterday.

（三）语法填空

阅读下面材料，在空白处填入适当的内容（1个单词）或括号内单词的正确形式。

John：Hi, Mr. Green. ___1___ you give me a hand?

Mr. Green：Of course. You ___2___ hesitate to ask me for help. What's wrong with you?

John：My parents always complain about my getting up late on weekends.

Mr. Green：When do you usually get up?

John：I usually get up at noon. But I know that I ___3___ get up earlier.

Mr. Green：Why don't you get up earlier?

John：My parents usually say, "Everyone ___4___ have a healthy lifestyle and get up early, and that is a basic rule for all of us." You see, if I got up earlier, I ___5___ have a good rest and relax. I am so tired.

Mr. Green：Both you and your parents are reasonable. As parents, they believe that you ___6___ get up earlier and develop a healthy lifestyle, while you think you need more time to have a good rest. Do your parents know what you think?

John：No. Even if I had told them before, they ___7___ have understood it.

Mr. Green：I don't think you are right. I think you should tell your parents what you think and they would understand you. Besides, you had better not hide your feelings from your parents and you ___8___ as well learn to communicate with them.

John：Thank you for your advice. It is high time I ___9___ （talk） with them.

Mr. Green：I ___10___ agree more.

（四）短文改错

Dear Mr. Green,

We are planning to launch a voluntary activity next month, which theme is protecting endangered wild animals. I am writing to ask your permission to held an exhibition next month. As you known, a great number of wild animals had been in danger. That is why we needn't take immediate action to protect them. We must like to hold the exhibition in front of the teaching building where a lot of pictures would be shown to remind us what serious challenges wild animals are faced with and what we should do to help them. Hopefully it can to help arouse our awareness of animal protection.

I would appreciate it if you will take my request into consideration.

Looking forward to you early reply.

Yours,

Li Hua

第十章 虚拟语气

英语中有三种语气，即陈述语气、祈使语气和虚拟语气。陈述语气用来陈述事实；祈使语气用来表示请求、命令、劝告和指示等；虚拟语气用来表示假设、建议、要求、主张等，强调一种假想的情况或主观愿望，虚拟语气中的动词时态用法比较特别，往往会与现在事实情况相反、与过去事实情况相反以及与将来事实情况可能相反，学习中要特别注意动词的形式。

一、含有虚拟语气的主从复合句

情况	从句时态	主句时态
与现在情况相反	were（各人称）/ did	would / should / could / might +do
与过去情况相反	had done	would / should / could / might+ have done
与将来情况相反	1.did 2.were（各人称）to do 3.should do	would / should / could / might + do

If you **were** tears in my eyes, I **would** never **cry**, because I'm afraid I'll lose you.

如果你是我眼睛里的泪水，我永远不会哭，因为我担心会失去你。

If I **had met** you yesterday, I **would have told** you the news.

如果我昨天遇见你的话，我就把那个消息告诉你了。

If it **should rain** / **rained** / **were to rain** tomorrow, the crops **would be saved**.

如果明天下雨的话，庄稼就会得救。

If you **had followed** my advice then, you **would be** a university student in Grade Two now. （混合主从复合句）

如果你当初听我的建议的话，你现在就是大二的学生了。

当从句中有were，had，should 时，把这些词提到句首，省略if，形成倒装句。例如：

Were I your daughter，I would be very happy，because you can teach me English every day.

如果我是你的女儿，我会很高兴，因为你可以每天教我学英语。

Had it not been your help，I wouldn't have succeeded.

要不是有你的帮助，我不会成功的。

Should the weather become better，we would go climbing this afternoon.

天气要变得好点的话，我们下午就去爬山。

二、其他情况下的虚拟语气

（1）wish后的宾语从句以及if only后的句子要用虚拟语气。与现在事实相反用过去时，与过去事实相反用过去完成时，与将来事实可能相反用would / could加动词原形。例如：

I wish that I **had** a lot of money now.

但愿我现在有很多钱。

I wish that he **had passed** the examination yesterday.

但愿他昨天通过考试就好了。

I wish that I **would**（**could**）**fly** to the moon one day.

但愿有一天我能飞上月球。

If only I **were** 20 years younger.

我要是年轻20岁就好了。

If only I **had met** you yesterday.

我昨天要是遇见你就好了。

If only I **would / could** go to Cambridge University next year.

我明年要是能上剑桥大学就好了。

（2）prefer，would rather后的句子要用虚拟语气。与现在事实相反用过去时，与过去事实相反用过去完成时，与将来事实可能相反多用过去时，偶尔也用should加动词原形。例如：

I prefer you **were** much stronger and taller.

我宁愿你更强壮更高。

I prefer you **had attended** my lecture last time.

我宁愿你上次来听我的讲座。

I prefer you **came** alone tomorrow afternoon.

我宁愿你明天下午一个人来。

I would rather you **were** an English speaker, and then we can communicate more easily.

我宁愿你会讲英语，那我们交流就更容易了。

I would rather you **had learned** English when you were at school.

我宁愿你上学时就学过英语了。

I would rather you **studied** harder next semester.

我宁愿你下学期更加努力地学习。

（3）表示"要求、主张、建议、命令"的动词，与之相关的名词性从句中都用should+动词原形，should 可以省略。这些动词通常是两个主张——insist，urge，三道命令——order，command，adjure，四个建议——suggest，advise，propose，recommend，五个要求——desire，demand，ask，require，request。

试翻译：

他提出建议，那个女孩应该被派到西藏去工作。

He suggested that the girl （**should**）**be sent** to work in Tibet.（宾语从句）

It's suggested that the girl （**should**）**be sent** to work in Tibet.（主语从句）

His suggestion is that the girl （**should**）**be sent** to work in Tibet.（表语从句）

He put forward the suggestion that the girl （**should**）**be sent** to work in Tibet.（同位语从句）

The boss ordered that all the goods （**should**）**be put** in proper places.

老板命令，所有的货物都应该放在合理的地方。

My teacher recommended that we （**should**）**buy** at least two dictionaries each.

我的老师推荐我们每人至少买两本字典。

Our school regulation requires that all the students（should）wear school uniforms whenever we are at school.

我们学校的规定要求，所有学生只要在学校就得穿校服。

但如果suggest表示"暗示，表明"时，insist表示"坚持说某个事实"时，不用虚拟语气，而要用相应的正确时态。例如：

The smile on his face suggested that he was happy to have given his life for his country.

他脸上的微笑表明，他很高兴为祖国献出自己的生命。

The doctor insisted that he had been badly injured and that he （should）be operated on at once.（insist后接两个宾语从句，第一句中insist是"坚持说某个事实"，第二句中是"主张"）

医生坚持说他伤势很重，并且主张应该立刻做手术。

（4）as if，as though引导的方式状语从句中用虚拟语气，与现在事实相反用过去时，与过去事实相反用过去完成时。例如：

She treats me in that way as if I were her father.

她对待我的方式，就仿佛我是她爸爸似的。

He talks about America as if he had been there before.

他谈论起美国就仿佛他以前去过那儿似的。

（5）It's time that...后的从句中多用过去时，也可用should+动词原形表示虚拟语气。例如：

It's high time that we went to school. = It's high time that we should go to school.

我们该去上学了。

（6）It's natural / important / strange / necessary / desirable / surprising / no wonder that...句型中，谓语动词用should + 动词原形。例如：

It's necessary that we should learn how to use a computer.

我们学习如何使用电脑是必要的。

It's strange that tourists should never go and visit that mysterious place.

奇怪的是游客竟然从来不去参观那个神秘的地方。

Many people think it important that students should take part in some social practice.

很多人认为学生参加社会实践活动是重要的。

（7）在so that / in order that / in case / for fear that 引导的状语从句中用虚拟语气。例如：

He got up early **so that / in order that** he could catch the first bus.

他早早起床以便能够赶上第一班公共汽车。

Bring some warm clothes **in case** you（should）need them while you are there.

带上暖和的衣服，以防你在那边的时候需要它们。

三、虚拟语气的特殊情况

（1）有时候不用if引导的从句表示条件，而是用介词、副词、分词短语等的含蓄条件。例如：

But for（**Without**）your help，I wouldn't have succeeded.

要不是你的帮助，我不会成功的。

He didn't follow my advice，**otherwise** he would have passed the driving test.

他不听我的建议，否则他会通过驾驶测试的。

Given more time，he could have done it better.

多给点时间的话，他会做得更好。

（2）would like to have done 表示"过去想做但没做成"。例如：

I **would like to** have come to your birthday party，but I had something urgent to do.

我本想来参加你的生日宴会，但有急事要做。

——**Did** you participate in the English-speaking competition last week?

你上周参加英语演讲比赛了吗?

——I **would like to** have，but I was not allowed to.

我也想，但他们不让我这么做。

（3）动词think，believe，plan，intend，hope，mean等的过去完成时可以表示未曾实现的愿望或想法。例如：

I **had thought** the room to be empty but it was occupied actually.

我原以为这间屋子是空的，但事实上被占了。

I **had meant** to come to your birthday party，but something unexpected happened.

我原打算来参加你的生日宴会，但一些出乎意料的事发生了。

（4）用在表示祝愿的句子中。例如：

Long live the Communist Party of China! 中国共产党万岁!

May you have a healthy and long life! 祝你健康长寿!

Exercise Ten

（一）单句语法填空

1. The doctor recommended that you _____ swim after eating a large meal.

2. If I _____ （receive） your letter, I would have set off two days ago.

3. Mr. White_____ （arrive） at 8：30 for the meeting, but he didn't turn up.

4. _____I to do the work, I should do it in another way.

5. She wished that she_____ （pass） the examination next time.

6. Miss Zhang requested that her students_____ （be） on time for every class.

7. If I should have time, I_____ （go） to the theatre tomorrow evening.

8. It's high time that we students_____ （work） even harder at our lessons as the national entrance examination is coming near.

9. Mary_____ （grow） much taller, but her cruel stepmother never let her eat enough.

10. Long_____ （live） the Communist Party of China!

（二）单句改错

1. Mary, can you post the letter for me if you went to the post office?

2. If I have a pair of wings, I could fly freely like a bird in the sky.

3. If I were you, I will plant some flowers and trees in the little garden.

4. I wish I can do something to make everyone live in a beautiful world.

5. If you worked hard then, you would be in the university now.

6. We would have a happier time during high school if there is less homework.

7. Peter wishes that he is a bit taller because he is very short, which is often laughed at by his classmates.

8. You have come earlier. The bus left a moment ago.

9. If I am the ruler of the world, I would make it a better place.

10. If only you hasn't offended him the other day!

（三）语法填空

阅读下面材料，在空白处填入适当的内容（1个单词）或括号内单词的正确形式。

American English has its own idioms. Let's say you buy something in a shop. ___1___ you pay for it, you say, "This costs ___2___ （I）an arm and a leg！" What do you really mean by ___3___ （say）so? Do you have to give them your arm and leg? I hope not. Let's listen to an American English conversation ___4___ （see）if we can find out what this means.

A：Did you buy that new computer?

B：Yeah, I did. But I shouldn't ___5___ （buy）it.

A：Why do you say so? Is there anything wrong with it?

B：Not exactly. But as a matter of fact, it cost me the way more than I ___6___ （expect）it to be.

A：How ___7___ did you pay for it?

B：It cost an arm and a leg!

When you say in American English that something costs an arm and a leg, it actually means that ___8___ price is very, very high, much ___9___ （high）than you can accept. If you use this idiom in the United States, everyone there ___10___ （understand）you. But this is an informal phrase, so don't use it in a formal business setting.

（四）短文改错

The summer holiday is coming. My classmates and I are talking about how to do during the holiday. We can chose between staying at home and take a trip. If we stay at home, it is comfortable but there is no need to spend money. But in that case, we will learn little about world. If we go on a trip abroad, we can broaden your view and gain knowledge we can get from books. Some classmates suggest that we can go to places of interest nearby. I thought that it is a good idea. It does not cost many, yet we can still learn a lot.

第十一章　非谓语动词

现行高中英语教材把非谓语动词分为动词不定式、动词-ing形式以及过去分词三部分。为了便于学生学习，本书把非谓语动词分为动词不定式、分词和动名词。所谓非谓语动词就是由动词变化而来但不能作谓语的几种形式，但它们可以带自己的宾语或者状语，构成非谓语动词短语。下面分别来介绍它们的用法。

一、动词不定式

1. 动词不定式的功能

动词不定式具有名词、形容词和副词的特征，同时保留动词的特征，因此可以有自己的宾语和状语，构成不定式短语，在句中作主语、宾语、定语、状语、补语、表语。例如：

（1）作主语：

To be a key university student is my long-time dream.

成为重点大学的学生是我多年的梦想。

To love and to be loved are both happiness.

爱和被爱都是幸福。

第一，动词不定式作主语时经常用it作形式主语，动词不定式作真正主语，通常有下列几种句型：

It is very nice to be independent.

不依靠别人是非常好的。

It is a great pleasure to be together with you.

跟你在一起真是件愉快的事情。

It usually takes me four or five hours to finish my daily task.

完成我的日常任务通常要花四五个小时。

It is beyond my power to answer such a difficult question.

回答如此难的问题超出我的能力。

It's not easy for me to learn English well.

对我来说，学好英语不容易。

It's very kind of you to help me with my English.

=You are very kind to help me with my English.

你帮助我学习英语，你真好。

第二，动词不定式的逻辑主语可以用of引出，也可以用for引出。用for引出动词不定式的逻辑主语时，它前面的形容词往往说明动词不定式的性质，而不是说明逻辑主语，常用的形容词有：important，necessary，difficult，hard，easy等；而of引出动词不定式的逻辑主语时，经常连用表示人的品质的形容词，常用的形容词有：nice，good，cruel，typical，silly，foolish，stupid，bright，clever，wise，right，wrong，mistaken等，也可以用"逻辑主语+系动词+该形容词"模式改写，句意通顺。例如：

It is quite necessary for us to fasten our safety belts while we are driving.

对我们来说，开车时系上安全带是相当必要的。

It was silly of her to believe him. = She was silly to believe him.

她真是愚蠢，竟然相信他。

（2）作宾语：

第一，动词agree，beg，choose，decide，afford，fail，expect，hope，long，offer，manage，plan，prepare，pretend，strive，refuse，intend，promise，seem，wish，want等后面通常跟动词不定式作宾语，为了帮助大家记忆，我们把这些动词编成顺口溜：**同意乞讨选决定，付起失败期希望，渴望帮助管计划，准备假装努力抗，打算承诺似想要。**动词不定式一般不作介词宾语，但可以作but，except等介词的宾语。例如：

My parents promised to buy me a new computer as soon as I passed the exam.

我父母答应只要我通过考试就给我买台新电脑。

He had no choice but **to go home**.

他除了回家别无选择。

She had no alternative but **to walk home** because there were no buses or taxis in the street.

她除了走回家别无选择，因为街上没有公共汽车和出租车了。

第二，动词like，love，hate，continue等后面跟动词不定式和动名词作宾语时意义比较接近，其区别就在于不定式表示较具体的动作，而动名词则表示抽象概念。例如：

I like **swimming**, but I don't like **to swim** in that small pool with you this afternoon.

我喜欢游泳，但我不喜欢今天下午和你一起在那个小池子里游泳。

第三，动词begin，start在三种情况下只跟动词不定式作宾语：跟表示心理活动的动词，动词本身用于进行时，主语为物的时候。例如：

Then she began **to realize** that it was her best friend that betrayed her.

然后她意识到，是她最好的朋友出卖了她。

He was starting **to study** hard as soon as he got there.

他一到那儿就开始努力学习。

The deep ice began **to melt** as the weather became warmer and warmer.

随着天气越来越暖，厚厚的冰开始融化。

第四，不定式作宾语时，可以用it作形式宾语，it后常跟形容词或者名词作宾语补足语。例如：

I think it necessary and important **to learn English well** if you go abroad.

你如果出国，我认为学好英语是必要而且重要的。

We have made it a rule **to get up early and read English aloud every day**.

我们已经把每天早起和大声朗读英语定为规矩。

（3）作定语：

第一，动词不定式作定语时，要注意不定式跟被修饰词之间逻辑上的关系，通常会有"主谓关系""动宾关系"等。例如：

He is always the first **to come** and the last **to go**.（主谓关系）

他总是第一个来最后一个走。

He was the very person **to help** me when I was in trouble. （主谓关系）

他正是我处于麻烦之中时帮助了我的人。

Ladies and gentlemen! I have an announcement **to make** here. （动宾关系）

女士们，先生们！我这儿有一个通知要发布。

I have brought something important **to read**. （动宾关系）

我带了一些重要的东西来读。

第二，如果作定语的不定式中的动词不能跟被修饰的词之间构成动宾关系时，要加一个相应的介词，构成介宾关系，但介词的选择需合理。例如：

They want to build a big house to live **in**. （...live in a big house）

他们想盖一间大房子住。

I have brought a chair to sit **on**. （...sit on a chair）

我拿来了一把椅子要坐。

I have bought a pen to write **with**. （...write with a pen）

我买了一支写字用的钢笔。

I have bought some paper to write **on**. （...write on some paper）

我买了一些写字用的纸。

I will go to Beijing. Do you have anything **to be taken** there?

我要去北京。你有东西要捎过去吗？

注意：此句中you不是不定式的逻辑主语，所以anything就变成逻辑主语了，anything跟take构成被动的主谓关系，所以用不定式的被动式，但现代英语中也可用主动形式。例如：

I will do some washing. Do you have any clothes **to wash**（to be washed）？

我要洗衣服。你有衣服要洗吗？

There is a lot of homework **to be done** today. =There is a lot of homework **to do** today.

今天有很多作业要做。

第三，某些抽象名词如ability，way，need，possibility，determination等后也可跟不定式作定语。例如：

The system has the ability **to run** more than one program at the same time.

这个系统有同时运转一个以上项目的能力。

The way **to solve** the problem has not been found.

解决这个问题的办法还没找到。

He has showed the determination **to succeed** in the coming exam.

他已经表现出了在即将到来的考试中成功的决心。

（4）作状语：

动词不定式作状语时，通常表示原因、目的和结果等，它的逻辑主语通常是句子的主语，有主动和被动之分，大家在学习和运用中要特别注意。例如：

I was very pleased **to get** the good and exciting news.（原因）

因为得到那个令人兴奋的好消息，我很高兴。

In order to learn English well，I have to buy a good dictionary.（目的）

为了学好英语，我不得不买一本好字典。

She changes her clothes every day **so as to be noticed** by others.（目的，so as to 不能置于句首）

她每天都换衣服以便能被别人注意到。

The question is very difficult **to answer**.

=**To answer the question** is very difficult.

这个问题回答起来很难。

注意：动词不定式在这种情况下作状语时，一般是及物动词，跟主语之间是逻辑上的动宾关系，往往翻译为"……起来"，不用被动形式。例如：

The man is very hard **to deal with.**=**To deal with the man** is very hard.

这个人对付起来很难。

Exciting as its special effects are **to watch**，there is too much violence in the film.

=Although its special effects are exciting **to watch**，there is too much violence in the film.

= Although **to watch** its special effects is exciting，there is too much violence in the film.

尽管这部电影的特技效果看起来很令人兴奋，但还是有太多暴力。

He came to the classroom，**only to find** there were no students in it.（出乎意料的结果）

他来到教室，出乎意料地发现教室里没学生。

He hurried to the airport，**only to be told** that the movie star had left.（出乎意料的结果）

他匆匆赶到机场，结果有人告诉他说，那位电影明星已经走了。

注意：分词也可作结果状语，但与动词不定式有区别，不定式的主动和被动形式都表示出乎意料的结果，现在分词和过去分词均表示必然结果。例如：

He was late again and again，**thus making** the class teacher very angry.（必然结果）

他一次次迟到，这样就必然使班主任生气。

He smoked again and again while working，**thus caught** by the boss.（必然结果）

他上班时一次次吸烟，这样必然就被老板抓住。

（5）作宾语补足语或主语补足语：

第一，作宾语补足语（以下简称宾补）或主语补足语（以下简称主补）时，不定式的逻辑主语就是宾语或者主语，有主动和被动之分。下列动词常跟不定式作宾补：advise，allow，ask，beg，cause，consider，desire，encourage，expect，force，get，invite，oblige，order，permit，persuade，prefer，request，teach，tell，want，warn等。例如：

Our school doesn't allow anyone **to smoke**.

我们学校不容许任何人吸烟。

They forbid the books **to be taken** out of the library.

他们禁止将书带出图书室。

We were forced **to leave** the classroom as soon as the bell rang.

铃一响，我们就被强迫离开教室。

She was persuaded **to be sent** to work in Tibet.

她被说服去西藏工作。

第二，动词或短语notice，let，make，hear，listen to，see，look at，watch，observe，have，feel等后跟省略to的动词不定式作宾补，但上述动词或

短语变为被动语态时，作主补的不定式要加上to。这些动词可以用这样一句话来记忆："注意让迈克听听看看这块表有啥感觉。"例如：

I noticed a lady **enter** the classroom.

我注意到一位女士进了教室。

A lady was noticed **to enter** the classroom.

有人注意到一位女士进了教室。

第三，这些动词后既可跟省略to的不定式也可跟现在分词作宾补，区别在于：现在分词侧重当时的情景，动作未必完成，而不定式侧重整个动作过程。例如：

I saw the boys **playing** near the river.

我看见男孩们在河边玩。

I saw a boy **fall off** the bicycle in the street.

我在街上看见一个男孩从自行车上掉了下来。

（6）作表语：

动词不定式作表语既可表示将来发生的动作，也可表示应该做某事。例如：

In such dry weather, the flowers will have to be watered if they are **to survive**.

在如此干燥的气候条件下，要想这些花活下来，就得给它们浇水。

Who is **to blame** for the broken window？ （blame在这个用法中常用主动形式表被动）

窗户被打破了，谁应该受到责备？

2. 动词不定式的时态和语态

时态	主动形式	被动形式
一般式	to do	to be done
完成式	to have done	to have been done
进行式	to be doing	无
完成进行式	to have been doing	无

动词不定式不仅有时态的变化，而且有语态的变化。当不定式的逻辑主语是不定式所表示的动作的承受者时，就要用被动语态。

（1）不定式的一般式表示动作或状态与谓语动词动作或状态同时发生或之后发生。例如：

He likes **to swim** in the Yellow River.

他喜欢在黄河里游泳。

Nobody likes **to be criticized** in public.

没有人喜欢在公共场所被批评。

（2）不定式的完成式表示动作或状态在谓语动词动作或状态之前发生。例如：

I'm glad **to have met** you at such an important place.

真高兴在这么重要的地方见到了你。

The book is said **to have been translated** into many languages.

据说这本书已经被翻译成了很多种语言。

（3）不定式的进行式表示动作在谓语动词动作或状态发生时正在发生。例如：

He pretended **to be sleeping** when his mother entered his room.

妈妈进来他房间的时候他假装正在睡觉。

（4）不定式的完成进行式表示在谓语动词动作或状态发生之前开始的动作，到谓语动词动作发生时可能停止，也可能会持续下去。例如：

He seems **to have been whitewashing** the walls for five hours.

他似乎已经刷墙有五个小时了。

He is said **to have been sitting** there for at least four hours.

据说他在那儿坐了至少四个小时了。

3. 动词不定式的其他问题

（1）不定式的否定形式是在不定式符号to前面加not构成的。例如：

The teacher asked us **not to make** any noise in the classroom.

老师要求我们不要在教室内吵闹。

The teacher warned us **never to give up** before difficulties.

老师告诉我们在困难面前不要放弃。

（2）疑问词 + 不定式：

"疑问词 + 不定式"结构相当于一个名词，在句中可作主语、宾语和表语，其中的不定式通常要用一般式。例如：

How to deal with the problem has caused a heated discussion.（作主语）

如何处理这个问题已经引起了一场热烈的讨论。

If you don't know **when to start**，you'd better call him.（作宾语）

如果你不知道什么时候开始，你最好给他打电话。

The problem is **what to do** next in such a confusing situation.（作表语）

问题是在这样混乱的局势下，下一步该做什么。

（3）不定式符号to的省略情况：

第一，在had better，would rather...than...，would...rather than...，do nothing but / except / other than，might as well，cannot help but / cannot choose but / cannot but以及情态动词、助动词之后都用省略to的不定式，即动词原形。例如：

I would rather **stay** at home than **go** to the cinema in such terrible weather.

在这么恶劣的天气情况下，我宁愿待在家里而不去看电影。

In this case，there is nothing I can **do** other than / but / except **go** home.（前面有do的任何形式，后面省略to）

在这种情况下，我除了回家别无选择。

She cannot choose but **drop** out of school because of poverty.

由于贫穷她只得辍学。

第二，动词或短语notice，let，make，hear，listen to，see，look at，watch，observe，have，feel后跟不定式作宾补时要省略to。例如：

The boss made his employees **work** more than 10 hours a day.

那位老板使员工每天工作10个小时以上。

The woman teacher has her students **finish** 10 exercises each day.

那位女教师让学生每天做完10个练习。

第三，动词help后可直接跟省略to的不定式，即help do sth.，help后的不定式作宾补时，如果句子主语直接参与不定式动作则省略to，句子主语不直接参与不定式动作，一般不省略to。例如：

Then the monitor **helped clean** the classroom and the passage outside the classroom.

然后班长帮着打扫了教室以及教室外面的走廊的卫生。

Would you please help me **carry** the box upstairs?

请帮我把箱子扛到楼上好吗?

The book will help you **to improve** your English.

这本书会帮你提高你的英语水平。

第四,在以why 或why not开头且表示建议的疑问句中用省略to的不定式。例如:

Why **argue** with a gossip when you can keep silent?

当你能保持沉默时,为什么跟长舌妇争吵呢?

Why **not try** opening the back door when you cannot open the front door?

当你不能打开前门时,为什么不尝试打开后门?

第五,并列的两个以上的不定式,从第二个开始省略to,但对比关系中不能省略。例如:

She will come to see us and **help** us with the project and solve some problems next month.

下个月她将来看我们、帮助我们做项目并且解决一些问题。

We haven't decided whether **to go** abroad or **to stay** in China during the vacation. (表比较)

我们还没有决定假期要出国还是待在中国。

第六,系动词前面有动词do的任何形式,句子主语是all或what引导的从句,或者主语被only,first,one,least及形容词最高级所修饰时,作表语的不定式可以省略to。例如:

The first thing I want to do now is(**to**) **thank** all the people who have helped me in my life.

此刻我想做的第一件事就是感谢我生命中所有帮助过我的人。

All I can do at present is(**to**) **offer** him some money to buy food and clothes.

目前我能做的一切就是给他一点买食物和衣服的钱。

What she really hopes is(**to**) **marry** a kind and honest man.

她真正希望的就是嫁一个友善诚实的人。

The only thing he can do now is(**to**) **study** hard and do well in the exam.

他现在唯一能做的就是努力学习考好试。

第七，在一些固定短语中不用to，如I dare say（我敢说），let go（放开，松手），make do（凑合，应付），make believe（假装）等。例如：

I **dare say** you didn't pay much attention to what you were doing.

我敢说你没有对所做的事情给予太多留意。

Don't **let go** on the halfway when you climb up the hill.

你在攀岩半道别松手。

It may not be a great suggestion. But before a better one is put forward，let's **make do** with it.

这个建议也许不好。但在更好的建议提出之前，让我们先凑合一下吧。

Children like to **make believe** that they are teachers at home.

孩子们在家里喜欢假装他们是老师。

二、分词

1. 分词的功能

分词包括现在分词和过去分词，现在分词表示主动同时，过去分词表示被动完成，均具有形容词和副词的特征，因此在句中作定语、表语、补语和状语。

（1）作定语：

第一，单个分词一般作前置定语，分词短语作后置定语。**现在分词完成式不作定语**。例如：

China is a **developing** country while America is a **developed** country.

中国是一个发展中国家而美国是一个发达国家。

The man **standing over there** is the man **injured in the accident last year**.

站在那儿的那个人就是去年在事故中受伤的那个人。

第二，单个过去分词作定语时有三种情形：只表被动、只表完成、既表被动又表完成。例如：

You should be not only good at **written** English but also **spoken** English.（只表被动）

你不仅应该擅长书面英语而且应该擅长口头英语。

She drank some **boiled** water after she cleared away some **fallen** leaves.（不及物动词只表完成）

她清理完落叶后喝了一些凉开水。

Can you see the **broken** glass on the ground? （既表被动又表完成）

你能看见地上被打破的玻璃吗？

第三，过去分词短语作定语表被动完成，必须后置，相当于一个定语从句；单个过去分词作定语要前置，但left经常后置，表示被动。例如：

The first textbooks **written** for teaching English as a foreign language came out in the 16th century.

= The first textbooks which **were written for** teaching English as a foreign language came out in the 16th century. （过去分词短语作限制性定语等于限制性定语从句）

第一批英语教科书在16世纪出版了。

The Olympic Games, first **played** in 776 BC, did not include women players until 1912.

=The Olympic Games, which **were first played** in 776 BC, did not include women players until 1912. （过去分词短语作非限制性定语等于非限制性定语从句）

奥运会直到1912年才允许女运动员参加，它最早是公元前776年开始的。

When we finished the task, there were still fifteen minutes **left**.

当我们完成任务时，还剩十五分钟时间。

She is going to buy a gift for her husband with the **remaining** 45 dollars. （remain 为不及物动词，作定语时只用现在分词形式）

她打算用剩下的四十五美元为丈夫买一个礼物。

第四，过去分词作后置定语且表示被动的非谓语有三种情形：现在分词被动式表示"正在被……"，过去分词表示"已经被……"，动词不定式被动式表示"将要被……"。例如：

The building **being constructed now** will be used as our teaching building.

现在正在建设的那栋楼将被用作我们的教学楼。

The building **completed last year** cost 20 million dollars.

去年竣工的那栋楼花了两千万美元。

The building **to be completed next year** will be the tallest building in our campus.

明年将要竣工的那栋楼将是我们校园内最高的楼。

（2）作表语：

分词作表语表示主语的特征，现在分词多用来说明物，经常翻译为"令人……"，而过去分词多用来说明人，经常放在系动词be，get，remain，stay等后面。例如：

The story is very **interesting and exciting**.

这个故事非常有趣，也令人兴奋。

The girl was **seated** at the back of the classroom，feeling **disappointed**.

那个女孩坐在教室后排，感到有点失望。

（3）作补语：

分词可作主语补足语和宾语补足语，它们的逻辑主语分别是句子的主语和宾语，现在分词与逻辑主语之间是主动关系，过去分词与逻辑主语之间是被动关系。常跟分词作宾补的动词有：find，catch，get，have，keep，leave，send，start以及感官动词和短语see，look at，hear，listen to，notice，watch，observe等。例如：

I left my friend **waiting** at the gate of the school.

我让我的朋友在校门口等我。

He was caught **smoking** twice at work and he was fired.

上班时他被发现抽烟两次，因此被开除了。

I found myself **surrounded** by a group of children.

我发现自己被一群孩子包围起来了。

The house was noticed **broken into** last night.

有人注意到那间房子昨晚被破门而入了。

（4）作状语：

分词作状语时，它的逻辑主语就是句子的主语，现在分词表示主动同时，过去分词表示被动完成。分词作状语一般可以表示时间、原因、条件、让步、伴随、方式、必然结果等。例如：

① 作时间状语：

Seeing from the hill，we saw a lot of trees in the park.

从山上看的时候，我们看见了公园里的许多树。

Seen from the hill，the park looks very beautiful.

从山上看的时候，那个公园看起来很漂亮。

② 作原因状语：

Being ill，she didn't go to the important meeting yesterday.

因为病了，她昨天没有去参加那个重要会议。

Deeply **moved** by what the boy did，she went to help those poor people.

因为被那个男孩做的事情深深感动了，她去帮助那些穷人。

③ 作条件状语：

Turning to the right at the second crossing，you will find the hospital.

第二个十字路口向右转，你将会发现那家医院。

Given more time，I could have done it better.

再多给点时间，我会做得更好。

④ 作让步状语：

Working day and night for a long time，they didn't fulfill their task.

尽管夜以继日地工作了好长时间，他们还没有完成任务。

Badly **treated** by the leader，he went on working hard as before.

尽管被领导恶劣对待，他还是像以前一样继续努力工作。

⑤ 作伴随状语：

The teacher walked into the classroom，**holding** a book in his hand.

老师走进教室，手里拿着一本书。

The teacher walked out of the classroom，**followed** by his students.

老师走出教室，后面跟着他的学生们。

⑥ 作方式状语：

Travelling by bicycle，they visited many places of interest in China.

他们骑车参观了很多中国的名胜古迹。

She walked alone on the campus，**lost** in thought.

她独自在校园里散步，陷入沉思。

⑦ 作必然结果状语：

He dropped the glass carelessly，**breaking** it into pieces.

他粗心地掉了玻璃杯，结果它摔成了碎片。

2. 现在分词的时态和语态、否定形式

分词的否定式是在最前边加not。过去分词只有一种形式，及物动词的过去分词既表被动又表完成，而不及物动词的过去分词只表完成；现在分词有一般式和完成式两种，及物动词的现在分词还有被动形式，见下表：

时态	主动语态	被动语态
一般式	doing	being done
完成式	having done	having been done

（1）现在分词一般式表示和句子谓语动词动作同时发生。例如：

Not knowing what to say, he stood there silently.

因为不知道该说什么，他一声不吭地站在那里。

Holding his head high, the boy walked out of the classroom.

那个男孩高昂着头，走出了教室。

The bridge being built now will be completed next month.

目前在建的那座桥将于下个月竣工。

Being repaired, the road cannot be used at present.

因为正在被修，那条路现在不能用。

Being watched by the teacher, the girl felt a little nervous.

因为正在被老师看着，那个女孩觉得有点紧张。

以上两句中分词的动作表示"正在被……"，所以用了这种结构，一般来说，现在分词一般式的被动结构很少用作状语。

（2）现在分词完成式表示在谓语动词动作之前发生，只作状语。现在分词完成式被动结构与过去分词不同的是：现在分词完成式表示在谓语动词动作之前明显完成，而过去分词也表被动完成，但没有明显的完成。例如：

Having finished his homework, he went to play football.

做完作业之后，他去踢足球了。

Having been translated into many languages, the book became a best-seller.

被翻译成很多种语言之后，这本书变成了一本畅销书。

3. 分词的其他用法

（1）连词+分词：

由when，while，if，unless，though，as if引导的状语从句的主语与主句的主语一致时，可以省略从句中的主语及其他成分，把谓语动词变成分词形式。当分词与主句的主语是主动关系时用现在分词，是被动关系时用过去分词，这种现象又称为状语从句的缩略。请大家注意：这种缩略习惯上只用现在分词一般式和过去分词两种形式，偶尔使用现在分词完成式。例如：

When **asked** what his profession was，he just kept silent.

当被问到他的职业是什么时，他只是保持沉默。

While **crossing** the street，you'd better look to the left，then to the right.

当过马路时，你最好先向左看，再向右看。

Don't speak until **spoken to**.

直到有人跟你说话，你再说话。

Though **lacking** money，her parents managed to send her to college.

尽管缺钱，但她父母还是设法把她送到大学学习。

If **given** more money，the boy couldn't have done such a silly thing.

如果给他多一点钱的话，这个男孩不会干出这等傻事。

He suddenly stopped as if **realizing** something wrong.

他突然停了下来，仿佛意识到哪儿错了。

Though **having lived** abroad for a long time，he still observes Chinese customs.

尽管在国外生活了好长时间，他仍然遵守中国习俗。

（2）垂悬分词：

分词作状语时，它的逻辑主语一般都是句子的主语，但有时候分词的逻辑主语不是句子的主语，但在主句中能找到它的主语，这样的分词称为垂悬分词。例如：

Having suffered such heavy pollution，it may now be too late to clean up the **river**.

遭受了如此严重的污染之后，要把河流清理干净有点太晚。

Having stayed in the wild for such a long time，it might be difficult to make the boy adjust to human life.

在荒野中待了那么长时间以后，要让这个男孩适应人类生活也许有难度。

（3）分词的独立使用：

有些现在分词短语在句中作状语时，作独立成分，没有逻辑主语，也不考虑它跟句子主语之间的关系，常用的有：generally speaking，frankly speaking，strictly speaking，honestly speaking，personally speaking，broadly speaking以及judging by，judging from等。例如：

Generally speaking，English is a little easier to learn than Chinese.

一般来说，英语比汉语学起来容易一些。

Broadly speaking，women are easier to be persuaded to buy unnecessary things than men.

泛泛地讲，女人比男人更容易被说服买一些不必要的东西。

Judging from / by what he wears and has，he may be a very wealthy man.

根据他所穿的和拥有的东西来看，他也许是一个很富有的男人。

（4）用作介词的分词：

好多分词用作介词或连词，单独使用，不考虑与句子主语之间的关系，常见的有：according to，considering，following，including，owing to，supposing，providing，provided，given，seeing that，taking... into consideration / account等。例如：

According to what you said，he was not suitable for the job.

根据你所说的，他不适合做这项工作。

Considering his age and experience，he ought to be chosen for the position.

考虑到他的年龄和经验，他应该被选去干这个工作。

试比较：

Considered to be one of the best teachers，she was given a chance to take part in the competition.（分词作原因状语）

因为她被认为是最好的老师，所以给了她一次参赛的机会。

Everything considered，Tom was sent to volunteer in that school.（构成独立主格结构）

考虑到各种因素，汤姆被派到那所学校支教。

Following the college entrance examinations, a lot of research and investigation were done.

高考之后，人们做了好多调研。

There are 56 people in the classroom, **including** the teacher.

=There are 56 people in the classroom, **the teacher included**.（独立主格结构）

教室里有五十六人，包括老师。

He didn't come to the meeting yesterday **owing to** his serious illness.

由于病情严重，他昨天没来开会。

Supposing her unwillingness, what will you do then?

如果她不愿意，你该怎么办?

Supposing she doesn't come in time, we should start our second plan.

如果她不能及时来，我们应该启动第二套方案。

I will lend you $10,000 **providing / provided**（that）you pay it back at the end of the year.

你如果在年底以前还给我的话，我就借给你一万美元。

Given the general state of his health, it may take him quite a while to recover from the operation.

鉴于他健康的整体情况，要从手术中恢复过来还需要一段时间。

Seeing that everybody is here, let's begin our lesson.

既然大家都在这儿了，咱们开始上课吧。

Taking everything into consideration, we should work one more hour every day in order to finish the task on time.

考虑到各种因素，为了准时完成任务，我们应该每天多工作一个小时。

三、动名词

1. 动名词的功能

动名词具有名词的特征，但仍保留动词的性质，因此可以带自己的宾语、逻辑主语和状语，构成动名词短语，在句中作主语、宾语、表语和定语。

（1）作主语:

动名词及动名词短语作主语时，谓语动词通常用单数。当动名词短语较长时通常用it作形式主语，而动名词短语作真正主语，经常连用的词有use，useful，useless，good等。例如：

Watching English TV programs is a good way to learn English.

收看英文电视节目是学英语的一种好方法。

It is no use crying over spilt milk.

覆水难收。

It is good getting up early and reading English aloud every morning.

每天早晨早起大声朗读英语是件好事。

It is a waste of time talking about the matter without action.

光说不行动是浪费时间。

（2）作宾语：

① 作动词宾语：

有些动词和短语后只能跟动名词作宾语，常见的有：admit，allow，appreciate，advise，avoid，risk，celebrate，complete，consider，excuse，deny，escape，enjoy，suggest，forbid，miss，finish，imagine，keep，practice，mind，put off，insist on，give up，permit，keep on，be worth等，为了帮助记忆，我们把这些动词和短语编成顺口溜：承认允诺赏建议，避免冒险庆竣工，考虑借口否认逃，欣赏建议禁止错，结束想象保持练，介意推迟坚持戒，允许继续保价值。例如：

He is practicing playing the piano in the room upstairs.

他正在楼上房间里练习弹钢琴。

He has given up smoking and keeps running every morning.

他已戒烟并坚持每天早上跑步。

② 作介词宾语：

动名词作介词宾语时，一定要注意含有介词to的一些短语，如：lead to，devote to，look forward to，get down to，be used to，object to，stick to等。另有一些固定用法中，介词经常省略，如：have difficulty / trouble / problem / pleasure / fun / a good time / a bad time（in）doing，prevent / stop / keep sb. from doing，protect / guard / save / defend sb. from（against）doing，spend / waste...（in）doing，be busy（in）doing等。例如：

She is very good at **dancing** but she can't sing well.

她擅长跳舞，但唱歌不好。

The discovery of new evidence led to the thief **being caught**.（动名词复合结构）

新证据的发现导致那个小偷被抓。

She devoted her whole life to **studying and protecting** wild animals.

她一生致力于研究和保护野生动物。

It's time for us to get down to **reading** English aloud.

现在该我们开始大声朗读英语了。

He had no difficulty **finding** the professor's house because of his good sense of direction.

由于他方向感好，找到教授家没遇到困难。

The government must take measures to prevent people （from） **polluting** the environment.

政府必须采取措施阻止人们污染环境。

You'd better protect yourself from **being attacked** by bees.

你最好保护自己不受蜜蜂袭击。

We spend more than three hours **doing** our homework every day.

我们每天花三个多小时做作业。

Don't disturb him. He is busy **writing** a book these days.

别打扰他。他这些日子忙着写一本书呢。

③ 有些动词后跟动名词和不定式意义相同，区别仅在于：动名词表示概念或习惯性动作，而不定式表示具体动作。例如：

I like **reading**, but I don't like **to read** when I am tired.

我喜欢读书，但我不喜欢在疲倦的时候读书。

He loves **swimming**, but he doesn't love **to swim** in the small pool.

他喜爱游泳，但他不喜欢在这个小泳池里游泳。

We prefer **playing** basketball, but we prefer **to play** indoors rather than play outdoors.

我们偏爱打篮球，但我们宁愿在室内打而不是室外。

④ 有些动词和短语后跟动名词和不定式意义不同，如：remember，

forget，regret，try，mean，stop，go on，can't help等。例如：

I remember **meeting** you somewhere，but I am not sure where it is.（对做过的事还记得）

我记得在哪儿见过你，但我不确定在哪里。

Please remember **to turn off** the gas whenever you finish cooking.（记住去做某事）

请记住每次做完饭后关掉煤气。

I forgot **lending** you 100 dollars.（忘记做过的事了）

我忘了借给你100美元的事。

I forgot **to post** the letter for you.（忘记而没做，信还没有发出去）

我忘记替你发信了。

She regretted **telling** him the bad news.（对做过之事感到后悔）

她后悔告诉他那个坏消息。

I regret **to say / tell / inform / declare / announce** that we failed in the competition.（遗憾地要说某事）

我遗憾地说（告诉、通知、声明、宣布）我们在比赛中失败了。

Why not try **going** by water instead of by land? （试着做某事）

我们为什么不试着走水路而不走陆路呢？

We tried **to hear** what he said，but we couldn't.（设法做某事）

我们努力听他说什么，但没听见。

Missing a bus in some remote places means **waiting** for another day.（意味着做某事）

在一些偏僻的地方，错过一辆公共汽车就意味着还要等一天。

I am sorry I didn't mean **to hurt** you.（打算做某事）

很抱歉，我没打算要伤害你。

The baby girl stopped **crying** as soon as she heard her mother's voice.（停止所做之事）

那个女婴一听到妈妈的声音就停止哭泣了。

We stopped **to have** a rest when we covered half the distance.（作状语，停下来去做某事）

我们走了一半距离的时候停下来休息了一会儿。

After a short break, she went on **practising** playing the piano. (继续做同一件事)

短暂休息之后，她继续练习弹钢琴。

After we finished Unit One, we went on **to learn** Unit Two. (接着做另一件事)

我们学完第一单元之后，接着学习第二单元。

Hearing the bad news, they couldn't help **crying**. (情不自禁地做某事)

听到这个坏消息的时候，他们情不自禁地哭了。

I am very busy. I can't help **clean** the room now. (不能帮着做某事)

我太忙。我现在不能帮着打扫房间。

⑤ 动词need，want，require后跟动名词主动形式或不定式的被动式，表示"某事需要做"，这时候主语一般是物。例如：

My car needs / wants / requires **repairing**.

我的车子需要修理。

My shoes need / want / require **to be mended** now.

我的鞋现在需要修补。

（3）作表语：

动名词作表语时，相当于一个名词，表达主语的内容，通常可以把主语和表语互换；但现在分词作表语表示主语的特性，相当于一个形容词，所以前面可以加very，quite，extremely等副词修饰，但主语和表语不能互换。例如：

My hobby is **singing**.= Singing is my hobby.

我的爱好是唱歌。

My job is **teaching** children English.=Teaching children English is my job.

我的工作是教孩子们英语。

The film I saw last night is **very** exciting.

我昨晚看的电影非常令人兴奋。

My job is **quite** boring and tiring.

我的工作相当乏味且令人疲倦。

（4）作定语：

动名词作定语只有单个形式，放在被修饰的词之前，表示被修饰词的用途，通常可以用介词for去改写；而现在分词作定语表示被修饰词和分词之间逻辑上的主谓关系，相当于一个定语从句。例如：

a sleeping car = a car for sleeping 一节卧铺车厢（动名词）

a sleeping boy= a boy who is sleeping 一个睡觉的男孩（现在分词）

a swimming pool=a pool for swimming 一个游泳池（动名词，可加连字符）

a swimming girl= a girl who is swimming 一个游泳的女孩（现在分词，不能加连字符）

a running track=a track for running 一个跑道（动名词）

running water=water which is running 自来水（现在分词）

2. 动名词的时态、语态和否定形式

动名词的时态有一般式和完成式，动名词的语态有主动和被动之分，动名词的否定形式是在其前边加not。以动词do为例，见下表：

时态	主动	被动
一般式	doing	being done
完成式	having done	having been done

动名词一般式表示与谓语动词动作同时或稍后发生；而完成式表示动作先于谓语动词动作。如果逻辑主语是动名词的执行者就用主动形式，如果逻辑主语是动名词的承受者就用被动形式。例如：

He enjoys **listening** to the music and **singing** popular songs.

他喜欢听音乐和唱流行歌曲。

While shopping，some people，especially women can't help **being persuaded** to buy some unnecessary articles that they will never use.

购物时，一些人，尤其是女性会情不自禁地被说服买一些她们从来不用的没必要的东西。

I regret **having told** him the bad news without much thinking.

我不假思索地告诉他那个坏消息，我感到后悔。

He remembers **having been brought up** in the poor countryside.

他记得自己在贫穷的农村被抚养大。

3. 动名词复合结构

动名词复合结构就是动名词加自己的逻辑主语，这个逻辑主语通常用形容词性物主代词、名词所有格或者人称代词宾格、名词普通格。在句首和正式场合要用物主代词和所有格。如果逻辑主语是无生命物体、在句中或非正式场合多用人称代词宾格和名词普通格。动名词复合结构在句中作主语、宾语、表语。例如：

Tom's（His）**coming** late made us very unhappy.

汤姆（他）的迟到使我们非常不高兴。

The president's **attending** the meeting himself gave the students much encouragement.

校长亲自出席这次会议给学生们极大的鼓励。

Can you **imagine** Peter crossing the Atlantic within five days?

你能想象彼得在五天内穿过了大西洋吗？

At the **beginning** of the class, we could hear the noise of desks being opened and closed.

刚上课时，我们可以听到桌子被掀开和关上的声音。

His greatest excitement is his daughter **passing** the college entrance examination.

最令他激动的事是他女儿通过了高考。

What worried me most was I not being allowed to visit my mother in the hospital.

最使我担忧的是我不被容许在医院探视我的母亲。

四、独立主格结构和with复合结构

1. 独立主格结构

独立主格结构的构成：名词或者代词+名词（形容词、副词、介词短语、不定式、现在分词、过去分词），没有谓语动词，是一种具有逻辑主谓关系的短语，可以表达完整的意思，位置比较灵活。例如：

We met many foreign students in the school yesterday, **most of them Australians**.

我们昨天在学校里遇到很多外国学生，大部分是澳大利亚人。

I heard that my daughter got injured in the car accident, **my heart full of worry**.

我听说女儿在车祸中受伤，我的心里充满担忧。

Class over, all the students stood up and said thanks and good-bye to the teacher.

下课了，所有的学生站起来向老师说感谢和再见。

The teacher walked into the classroom, **book in hand**.（名词前不加限定词）

=The teacher walked into the classroom, **a book in his hand**.（名词前加限定词）

老师走进教室，手里拿着一本书。

注意：The teacher walked into the classroom, a book in hand.（错误）

The teacher walked into the classroom, book in his hand.（错误）

If no people to come to help us in time, we will have to leave the rest work till tomorrow.

如果没人及时来帮我们的话，我们不得不把剩下的工作留到明天。

More money to be provided, we will make the building more beautiful.

如果被提供更多钱的话，我们会把楼建得更漂亮。

It being Sunday, the students didn't come to school for class.

因为是星期天，所有学生都没来学校上课。

Weather permitting, we will go climbing the mountain tomorrow.

如果天气允许，我们明天去爬山。

The teacher having appointed homework for summer holidays, the students left the classroom.

老师布置完暑假作业之后，学生们离开了教室。

There being no bus or taxi, I had to walk home last night.

因为没有公共汽车和出租车了，昨晚我不得不走回家。

The thief was brought out of the mini-bus, **his hands tied behind his back**.

那个小偷被带下小面包车，手被绑起来放在背后。

They produced many cars last year, **most of them shipped abroad**.

他们去年生产了很多汽车，大部分运往国外。

2. with复合结构

with复合结构也是独立结构的一种，它的构成是：with / without+宾语+宾语补足语，其中宾语补足语可以用名词、形容词、副词、介词短语、不定式、现在分词以及过去分词充当，在句中可以作定语，但更多的是作状语。例如：

He quickly finished the work, **with his son a helper**.

有儿子做助手，他很快完成了工作任务。

Zhang Fei liked to sleep, **with his eyes wide open**.

张飞喜欢睁大眼睛睡觉。

With so many people around, I felt very shy to get changed. （around为副词）

周围有那么多人，我换衣服感到很害羞。

The lady **with a child in her arms** is from the countryside. （作定语）

怀里抱着小孩的那个女士来自乡下。

With agriculture and industry developing quickly, our life is becoming better and better.

随着工农业的飞速发展，我们的生活变得越来越好。

The war was over **without a shot being fired**.

一枪未发，战争就结束了。

She stood there, **with her eyes fixed** on the picture on the wall.

她站在那儿，眼睛盯着墙上的画。

With modern machines to do all the work, we will complete the construction ahead of time.

因为所有的工作都有现代化机械来做，我们将提前完成建筑任务。

独立主格和with复合结构中，动词不定式表示即将发生的动作，而现在分词表示正在进行或者已经发生的动作，与前面的名词之间构成逻辑上的主谓关系，否则就不是独立主格或with复合结构。例如：

With so many people **helping** us with our work, we have finished it ahead of time.

（helping表示已经在帮助，所以工作已经完成）

有那么多的人帮我们一起工作，我们已经提前完成了。

With so many people **to help** us with our work, I'm sure we can finish it ahead of time.

（to help表示将要帮助，因此工作即将完成）

因为有那么多人将要来协助我们工作，我确信我们能提前完成任务。

With so much homework **to do**, I daren't go to the cinema. （不定式作定语，非with复合结构）

有那么多的作业要做，我不敢去看电影。

With nothing **to do** in the office，he went home early.（不定式作定语，非with复合结构 ）

因为在办公室里没事可做，他早早就回家了。

Exercise Eleven

（一）单句语法填空

1. The flu is believed _____（cause）by viruses that like to reproduce in the cells inside the human nose and throat.

2. _____（visit）so many countries, you may have learned a lot about different cultures.

3. The purpose of developing new technology is to make life easier, _____（make）it more difficult.

4. _____（absorb）in his test papers, he didn't notice my coming.

5. I know I was not the first _____（arrive）, for I saw smoke _____（rise）from the window.

6. Eugene is never willing to alter any of his opinions. It's no use _____（argue）with him.

7. The flowers _____（smell）sweet in the botanic garden attract the visitors to the beauty of nature.

8. The news reporters hurried to the airport, only_____（tell）the film stars had left.

9. With time _____（go）by, Chinese people are proving that we can achieve what we want to the whole world.

10. _____（examine）twice a year, whether it is a car or a bus or a truck, is the rule that every driver must obey in this city.

（二）单句改错

1. When it comes to speak in public, no one can match him.

2. Lisa couldn't help, even though she tried not to, laughed at the fat boy.

3. It is usually cheaper to have the goods sending by sea than by air.

4. The agent promised to keep the family members fully informing of any development.

5. Shake her head, she said, "It isn't a good time to do that, dear."

6. But his parents think go to college is more important than playing sports.

7. My parents love me deeply of course and will do all they can make sure that I get a good education.

8. Losing in thought, he ran into a big tree and got hurt.

9. I came to realizing that life is equal to everyone.

10. After listening to his lecture, the students felt inspiring.

（三）语法填空

阅读下面材料，在空白处填入适当的内容（1个单词）或括号内单词的正确形式。

Scientists have discovered that ___1___ (stay) in the cold could help us lose weight. Researchers at the University of California found that exposure to the cold increases levels of a protein that helps form brown fat—the type of fat that produces heat and keeps us warm. Brown fat burns energy, ___2___ helps us lose weight. White fat stores extra energy, which results ___3___ weight gain. The researchers said that because air conditioning and heating give us constant, ___4___ (comfort) temperatures, our body's need for brown fat has decreased. They found that: "Outdoor workers in northern Finland who ___5___ (expose) to cold temperature have ___6___ significant amount of brown fat when ___7___ (compare) to the same-aged indoor workers."

The research was conducted on two different control groups of mice. ___8___ group was injected with the protein that helps create brown fat. This group later gained 30% less weight after both groups were fed high-fat diets. The researchers say this could be good news in the fight against obesity. People who are obese have ___9___ (low) levels of brown fat than thinner people. Head researcher Hei Sook Sul said,

"This protein could become an important target for research into the treatment and prevention of obesity and obesity-related diseases." She added, "If you can somehow increase levels of this protein, you could ___10___ (possible) lose more weight even if eating the same amount of food."

（四）短文改错

A woman crashed her car in an accident to avoid hit a squirrel on the road. The 82-year-old woman was driven along Washington Street toward Cass Avenue in Traverse, Michigan when she found a squirrel cross the road. The woman, who was driving a 2009 Ford Fusion, hit the side of a parking Honda CR-V, caused her car to flip upside down. A passer-by witnesses the crash and helped an elderly lady out of the vehicle. Emergency services arrived at the scene examine her. She was escaped with minor injuries. But officers issued her a ticket for driving with caution.

第十二章　状语从句

状语从句是贯穿于初中和高中阶段的一项语法，也是英语学习中最常见的语法现象。状语从句就是由从属连词引导的从句在句中作状语，修饰主句中的动词、形容词或者整个句子，可以置于主句之前，也可以在主句之后，放置句首时经常用逗号与主句隔开，可分为时间状语从句、地点状语从句、原因状语从句、条件状语从句、结果状语从句、目的状语从句、方式状语从句、比较状语从句和让步状语从句九种。

一、时间状语从句

（1）由when，as，while引导的时间状语从句。

第一，when表示"当……的时候"，既可以表示时间段，也可以表示时间点。例如：

I had to suffer from hunger and cold **when** I was a child.（when表时间段）

孩童时我不得不遭受饥饿和寒冷。

When he entered the classroom，all the students were reading.（when表时间点）

他进教室时，所有的学生都在读书。

when 还可以用作并列连词，意为and at that time suddenly，用来连接两个简单句成为一个并列句，常用于下列句式中：

I was doing my homework in the classroom **when** a terrible earthquake happened.

我正在教室做作业，这个时候突然一场可怕的地震发生了。

I was just about to leave the classroom **when** my class teacher came.

我刚打算离开教室，这个时候我的班主任来了。

I had just gone to bed **when** someone knocked at the door loudly.

我刚上床睡觉，这个时候有人大声敲门了。

第二，as表示动作的持续，常为"一边……一边……"。例如：

He sang the song **as** he ran along the street in the morning.

早晨，他一边沿街跑步一边唱着歌。

as也表"随着"，这时容易与with混淆。要注意：as是从属连词，引导一个句子；with是介词，后跟短语形式。试比较：

随着时间的推移，所有的学生都意识到学习英语的重要性。

With time goes on, all the students realize the importance of learning English.
（错误）

As time goes on, all the students realize the importance of learning English.
（正确）

With time going on, all the students realize the importance of learning English.
（正确）

第三，while引导的从句表示时间段，通常表示"在……期间"。例如：

I was watching TV in the sitting room **while** my mother was cooking in the kitchen.

当妈妈在厨房做饭的时候我在客厅看电视。

Please buy me some stamps **while** you are in the post office.

你在邮局时，请帮我买几张邮票。

while 在这种情况下是从属连词，引导一个句子，而during是介词，后跟名词性短语。试比较：

她在法国期间学了一点法语。

She picked up a little French **while** she stayed in France.

She picked up a little French **during her stay** in France.

while也可以用作并列连词，意为"而"，表示对比。例如：

In some places wives go out to earn money **while** their husbands stay at home, looking after children and cooking.

在有些地方，妻子在外赚钱而丈夫却待在家里照看孩子做饭。

（2）由as soon as, the moment, the minute, the instant, the second, immediately, directly, instantly, hardly...when, no sooner...than引导的时间状语

从句。这些引导词语均表示"一……就……"。例如：

The moment / minute / instant / second I saw her in the street, I recognized her.

在街上，我一看到她就认出了她。

She began to help her mother with cooking **immediately / directly / instantly** she arrived home after school.

放学后一回到家，她就开始帮妈妈做饭。

She had **hardly / no sooner** finished her homework **when / than** she went to the cinema.

她一做完作业就去看电影了。

Hardly / No sooner had he got into the room **when / than** the telephone rang.

他刚进屋子电话铃就响了。

注意：hardly，no sooner放在句首时，它们所在的句子要倒装且用过去完成时，而when，than所在的句子用一般过去时。

（3）由until，till引导的时间状语从句。在肯定的主句中要用延续性动词，表示动作到此时才结束；在否定的主句中要用短暂性动词，表示动作到此时才开始；句首只能用until；常用not...until...结构。例如：

A good storyteller must be able to hold his listeners' curiosity **until** he reaches the end of the story.

一个好的讲故事者必须一直抓住听众的好奇心直到故事讲完。

He **didn't** go to bed **until** his father came back that night.

那天晚上直到他父亲回来，他才去睡觉。

Until the person in charge comes, nothing can be done.

负责的人不回来，什么也不能做。

注意：not...until 在强调句型和倒装句中的不同，强调句型中不能用倒装，但要把not until都放在被强调部分。

试比较：

直到做完自己的工作，她才回家吃晚饭。

It was **not until** she finished her work that she went back home for dinner.（强调句型）

Not until she finished her work **did she go** back home for dinner.（倒装句）

（4）由before，after，since，once等连词引导的时间状语从句。

第一，before表示"在……之前"，还可以用作介词。

It won't be long **before** we take the final exams.

不久以后我们就要期末考试了。也可译为：在我们期末考试之前时间不会长了。

受汉语翻译影响，初学者容易在这种句型中犯错。实际上，before 引导的是时间状语从句，前面的句子是主句，也就是"在……之前有若干时间"。再如：

It will be a fortnight **before** they graduate from No.1 Middle School.

两周以后他们将从第一中学毕业。也可译为：在第一中学毕业之前还有两周时间。

The phone rang off **before** I could answer it.

我还没来得及接，电话就挂断了。也可译为：在我能接到电话之前它就挂断了。

注意：这个句式中，before仍然引导时间状语从句，表示"在能做某事之前……"，但通常会翻译为"在没有来得及之前……"，实际上从句中用的是肯定形式。

再如：

The earthquake was so terrible that all the houses fell down **before** citizens could escape.

这次地震如此凶猛，以至于居民没来得及逃出来房屋就倒塌了。也可译为：这次地震如此凶猛，以至于在居民逃出来之前房屋就倒塌了。

第二，since"自从……以来"，还可以用作介词，后跟名词性短语。

She has taught English in this school **since** she graduated from that normal university.

她从那所师范大学毕业以来一直在这所学校教英语。（一般而言，主句用现在完成时，从句用一般过去时）

It is / has been more than ten years **since** he left home.

自他离开家以来有十多年了。

在此句式中，从句中用短暂性动词表示"从那时开始到现在"，而用延续性或者状态性动词则表示"动作在那时终止"。例如：

It is twenty years **since** he began to smoke. （短暂性动词）

自他开始吸烟以来有二十年了。（他已有二十年的烟龄了）

It is nearly five years **since** she left home. （短暂性动词）

她离开家已经将近五年了。

It is twenty years **since** he smoked. （延续性动词，动作在二十年前终止）

他不吸烟有二十年了。

It is more than thirty years since I was a student. （状态性动词，状态在三十多年前终止）

我不是学生已经有三十多年了。

第三，once表"一旦"，与as soon as 容易混淆，但意义不同，前者带有"条件"意味，而后者表示两个动作的紧紧衔接。例如：

Once you see him，you will never forget him.

你一旦见他一面，你就不会忘掉他。

As soon as you see him，please give this note to him.

你一见到他就把这个便条给他。

第四，after 引导时间状语从句时可表动作发生的先后，故从句中没必要用过去完成时。例如：

He got married **after** he graduated from middle school.

他中学毕业之后就结婚了。

（5）由every time，each time，any time，the first time，the last time，by the time，the day，the time，the year等引导时间状语从句。例如：

Every time I was in trouble，he would come to help me.

每次我有麻烦时，他都会来帮我。

The first time I saw you，you were still a little baby.

我第一次见你时，你还是个婴儿。

He will have learned English for 8 years **by the time** he graduates next year.

到明年毕业为止，他学了8年的英语了。

The day he returned home，his father was already dead.

他回到家那天，他父亲已经去世。

The time we arrived at the village，it was already late evening.

我们到那个村子的时候，已经黄昏了。

（6）由whenever引导时间状语从句。例如：

Whenever he is free，he will go to help the old man.

无论什么时候有空，他都去帮助那位老人。

I will stay alone at home whenever I feel upset and unhappy.

无论什么时候我觉得不安和不快乐时，我都会独自待在家里。

注意：如果主句是将来时，时间状语从句中多用一般现在时、现在完成时等。

二、地点状语从句

（1）地点状语从句通常由where，wherever，anywhere，everywhere引导，可以放置主句之前，也可在主句之后。例如：

There used to be some trees where the high building stands today.

那栋高楼今天所在的地方过去有一些树。

Where there is confidence，there is success.

哪里有自信，哪里就有成功。（直译：成功就在有自信的地方。）

Trees can be planted wherever it rains a lot and it is warm.

树可以种在雨多暖和的任何地方。

Everywhere she went，she was warmly welcomed and received.

她所到之处，都受到热烈欢迎和热情接待。

We will go travelling anywhere you like.

你喜欢什么地方，我们就去什么地方旅游。

（2）where引导的地点状语从句和定语从句的区别：

定语从句中where之前有个表地点的名词作先行词，where 还可以被"介词+which"代替，但状语从句中where之前没有表地点的名词作先行词，where从句直接作状语。试翻译并比较：

待在原地不动。

Just stay in the place where you are and don't move.（定语从句）

Just stay where you are and don't move.（状语从句）

三、原因状语从句

（1）原因状语从句通常由because，as，since，now that等引导。because 语气最强，用来回答why 提出的问题，位置比较灵活，可以用于强调句型；as 语气较弱，引出较为明显的理由，多放置在句首；since 常放置在句首，引出双方已经知道的某个事实；now that 表示微弱的原因，用来说明一种新情况，然后加以推论。例如：

I was late for school this morning **because** my mother didn't wake me up in time.

我今天早晨上学迟到了，因为妈妈没有及时叫醒我。

It was **because** he helped me in time that I successfully fulfilled the task.（放在强调句型中）

因为他的及时帮助，我才成功完成任务。

As the weather was fine，I opened all the windows.

由于天气较好，我打开了所有的窗户。

Since everybody is here，let's have a discussion over the question.

既然大家都来了，咱们就讨论这个问题吧。

Now that you've got a chance，you might as well make full use of it.

既然你有机会，你不妨好好利用它。

（2）for 也可以表原因，但它是并列连词，构成并列句。语气很弱，不能放置在句首，往往引出一个"补充说明"，而不是直接理由。例如：

They might go out，**for** there is no light in the room.

他们也许出去了，因为屋里没灯光。（他们也可能没开灯或其他理由）

The day has broken，**for** the birds are singing.

天已经亮了，因为鸟在叫。（鸟不叫，天照样会亮的）

（3）because of，owing to，due to，thanks to，on account of 都可以用来表原因，但它们都是介词，后面只能跟名词性短语或what 引导的名词性从句。因为what = the things that...所以可以说because of后面还是跟了名词"the things+定语从句"。例如：

He didn't come to school yesterday **because of what** the monitor said（= the words that...）.

他昨天没来学校的原因是班长所说的话。

Owing to / Due to the bad weather，the sports meet was cancelled.

由于天气不好，运动会被取消。

Thanks to your timely help，I didn't get into trouble again.（thanks to表"好的理由"）

多亏了你的及时帮助，我没有再次陷入麻烦。

A survey indicates that，**on account of** the difficulty in finding a satisfactory job，many college students are in favor of running online shops.

调查表明，由于很难找到满意的工作，很多大学生支持经营网店。

（4）in that 实际上不是连词，而是介词in 后面跟了一个that 引导的宾语从句，当然也可以理解为"因为"。例如：

We were very lucky **in that** all the questions in the examination papers were familiar to us.

我们很幸运，因为试卷上所有的问题对我们来说都很熟悉。

She didn't attend the lecture given by the president **in that** she was badly ill.

她没有参加校长报告会，因为她病得很重。

（5）还有一个从句，有人认为是形容词的宾语从句，但也可以说成原因状语从句，因为这个从句说明前面形容词状态发生的原因。例如：

I am very happy **that** all of you have passed the examination.

你们大家都通过考试了，所以我很高兴。

She was extremely disappointed **that** her best friend didn't come to her birthday party.

她最要好的朋友没来参加她的生日宴会，所以她很失望。

四、条件状语从句

条件状语从句通常由so long as，as long as，on condition that，in case，if，unless，providing that，provided that，suppose，supposing等引导。当主句为将来时的时候，条件状语从句多用一般现在时或现在完成时。例如：

I will lend you some money **on condition that** you can return it to me in two months.

你如果能在两个月内还给我的话，我就借给你一些钱。

Send us a short message **in case** you have any difficulty.

万一有困难就给我们发短信。

Provided/Providing that you clear your desk by this evening, you can have tomorrow off.

如果你到今晚可以把手头上的工作做完，你明天就可以休息。

Suppose / Supposing we cannot find enough food，what shall we do?

假如不能弄到足够的食物，我们该怎么办？

五、结果状语从句

（1）结果状语从句通常由so that，so...that，such...that来引导。例如：

He got up very early this morning, **so that** he **caught** the first bus in time.（通常用逗号隔开，从句中用过去式）

他今天早晨起得很早，结果及时赶上了第一班公共汽车。

（2）当so that 引导的从句不用逗号与主句隔开，且从句中用情态动词could，might，can，would，may 等时，这个从句就是目的状语从句，也可以用in order that替换。例如：

He got up very early this morning **so that / in order that** he **could** catch the first bus in time.

他今天早晨起得很早以便能及时赶上第一班公共汽车。

（3）so... that，such... that 中that引导的是结果状语从句，具体用法如下：

第一，so + adj. / adv.+ that...

He runs **so fast that** nobody can catch up with him in our class.

他跑得如此快，以至于我们班没人能追上他。

第二，such + adj. + un.（不可数名词）

He has made **such great progress** in English that I can't help admiring him.

他在英语方面取得了如此大的进步，以至于我情不自禁地羡慕他。

第三，such + a + adj. + n.（可数名词）

It is **such a lovely day** that all the people would like to take a walk outside.

今天是一个如此好的天气，以至于所有人都想在外面散步。

第四，such + adj. + n.（pl.）（复数名词）

He has **such interesting books** at hand that he doesn't want to go to the cinema.

他手头有如此有趣的书，以至于他不想去看电影。

第五，so + adj. + a + n.= such + a + adj. + n.

Xi'an is **so beautiful a city** that thousands of visitors come for a visit every year.（也可以是such a beautiful city）

西安是如此漂亮的城市，以至于数以千计的人每年都来参观。

第六，当名词被many，few，much，little（少）修饰时，就要用so，不能用such。例如：

She has failed **so many times** that she dare not try again.

她失败过如此多次，以至于她不敢再次尝试。

Such a little child should make **so much money** but such a wise man should make **so little money**.（第一个little表示"小"，所以仍然用such，第二个little表示"少"，故用so）

如此小的孩子竟然赚如此多的钱，而如此聪明的大人却赚如此少的钱。

第七，so，such 包括所修饰的短语放置句首时，它们所在的句子要进行部分倒装。例如：

So attractive is the film that all the people would like to spend much time queuing for the tickets.

这部电影如此迷人，以至于所有的人都花时间排队买票。

Such a popular star is he that all the fans want to take a photo with him.

他是如此受人喜欢的一位明星，以至于所有的粉丝都想跟他合影。

注意：当such与不定代词all，no，some，any，few，several连用时，应该放在不定代词之后。例如：

All such possibilities must be considered ahead of time.

所有这些可能性都必须事先考虑到。

There is _____ person here as you described just now.

A. no such a   B. such no a   C. no such   D. such no

（正确答案：C。因为such 要放在no 之后，且no= not a，故A也不能选。）

六、目的状语从句

目的状语从句通常用so that，in order that，in case，for fear that引导，目的状语从句中经常用一些情态动词，如：can，could，may，might，should等，表虚拟语气。例如：

We lent her some money **so that / in order that** she **might** go on schooling.

我们借给她一些钱，以便她可以继续上学。

You had better leave the key at home in case one of us **should** think / thinks of coming back.

你最好把钥匙留在家里，以防我们中有人想回家。

七、方式状语从句

方式状语从句通常用as，as if，as though 引导，as if / as though 引导的方式状语从句中多用虚拟语气。例如：

You should do **as** your father tells you to.

你应该按照你父亲告诉你的去做。

He treats me in that way **as if** I were his father.

他对待我的方式，仿佛我是他父亲似的。

He talks about America **as though** he had been there himself.

他谈论起美国来就好像亲自去过那儿似的。

八、比较状语从句

比较状语从句通常用as...as，not as / so... as，than，the more... the more...，more... than引导。例如：

All the senior teachers try to do **as much as** the junior ones do in our school.

在我们学校，所有的老教师努力和年轻教师一样多地做工作。

The factory doesn't produce **so / as many** cars this year **as** last year.（否定句中才能用so，也可用as）

这个工厂今年生产的汽车不及去年多。

Her performance was **much** better **than** we expected.

她的表演比我们预期的要好得多。

The longer the period is，**the higher** the interest rate is.

周期越长，利率越高。

九、让步状语从句

（1）让步状语从句通常用although，though，while，however，whatever，whenever，whoever，no matter what...，whether，even if，even though 来引导。例如：

Although / Though he had been told again and again，he made the same mistake in the exam.

尽管有人一遍遍地给他讲，但他在考试中还是犯了同样的错误。

While I admit the fact that he is not perfect，I still love him very much.

尽管我承认他不完美这个事实，但我还是非常爱他。

However / No matter how hard he tried in everything，he didn't succeed in the end.

尽管在各方面努力了，但他最终还是没有成功。

No matter what / Whatever happens in the future，I will stand by you and help you out.

无论将来发生什么事，我都会支持你并帮你摆脱困境。

Whether it is fine or not，we will set off for the destination tomorrow morning.

无论天晴与否，我们明天早晨都向目的地出发。

Even if / Even though we can't get enough money，we shouldn't give up our plan.

即使我们不能弄到足够的钱，我们也不应该放弃计划。

（2）as 引导让步状语从句时要倒装，把句末的一个词以及修饰语放置句首，如果是单数可数名词时，把名词放置句首，冠词省略，though也有此用法。例如：

Very hard as / though he has been working, he hasn't succeeded so far.

尽管他非常努力地工作，但到现在为止他还没有取得成功。

Child as / though he is, he knows a lot about modern science and technology.

尽管他是个孩子，但他对现代科技知道得很多。

（3）在名词性从句中，只能用whatever，however之类的连词，但不能用no matter what，no matter who之类的连词。例如：

Whatever the teacher said in class this morning is worth thinking and discussing.

老师今早在课堂上说的一切都值得思考和讨论。

Whoever breaks the law should be punished seriously and equally.

无论谁犯法都应该受到公平严肃的惩罚。

（4）让步状语从句不能和but连用，因为but是并列连词，连接两个简单句，但可以用副词yet，still等。例如：

Although it is the first time for me to perform on this stage, **yet** I don't feel nervous.

尽管这是我第一次在这个舞台上表演，然而我不觉得紧张。

Though he has a great deal of money, **yet** he has never showed off.

尽管他有很多钱，但他从来没炫耀过。

（5）介词despite，in spite of 也表示"尽管"，但不能引导从句，只能跟名词性短语。例如：

Despite / In spite of the fact that he doesn't like foreign languages, he has to learn English well in order to find a good job in America.

尽管他不喜欢外语，但他不得不学好英语，以便在美国找到一份好的工作。

Despite / In spite of the bad weather, they continued to work in the fields.

尽管天气恶劣，但他们仍继续在田地里干活。

十、状语从句的缩略现象

为了使语言更加简洁、生动，在时间、条件、让步和比较状语从句中经常使用省略形式。省略要建立在主从句中的主语一致或从句中是it is / was结构时，省略后经常出现三种形式：第一，连接词+现在分词；第二，连接词+过去分词；第三，连接词+形容词或名词，现在分词完成时用得较少，几乎不用动词不定式。例如：

When **comparing** American English with British English, we find the differences in pronunciation, vocabulary and grammar.（comparing 与句子主语we之间是主动关系）

当我们比较美国英语和英国英语时，我们发现在发音、词汇和语法方面有差别。

When **compared** with the size of the whole earth, the biggest ocean doesn't seem big at all.（compared 与句子主语ocean之间是被动关系）

当和整个地球相比时，最大的海洋也一点都不显大。

If（it is）**possible**, please come and chat with me in my house.

如果可能的话，请来我家聊。

He will not come to the party, unless **invited**.（invited 与句子主语he之间是被动关系）

除非邀请，不然他不会来参加派对的。

No matter it rains or shines, the match will be held as **scheduled**.（scheduled 与句子主语match之间是被动关系）

无论下雨还是天晴，比赛都将按原计划举行。

Although **having achieved** considerable success as an outstanding basketball player, he keeps working hard after his retirement.（having achieved与句子主语之间是主动关系，且表示明显完成）

作为一名杰出的篮球运动员，他已经取得了相当大的成功，但退役之后他一如既往地努力工作。

Exercise Twelve

（一）单句语法填空

1. It gave him such a big shock _____ his face turned white suddenly.

2. We sent the letter by air mail _____（为了）it might reach them in good time.

3. He made a mistake, but then he corrected the situation _____（万一）it got worse.

4. We liked the oil painting _____（immediate）we looked at it.

5. When_____（compare）different cultures, we often pay attention only to the differences without noticing the similarities.

6. He tried his best to solve the problem, _____（无论）difficult it was.

7. I would appreciate it _____ you call back this afternoon for the doctor's appointment.

8. I had hardly got to the office _____ my wife phoned me to go back home at once.

9. _____ you go, don't forget your country.

10. Don't speak until _____（speak）to.

（二）单句改错

1. It is a long time after I saw you last time.

2. I was shopping at Folry's while I met an old friend.

3. She has made great progress than we expected.

4. He asked me not to move and stay which I was.

5. I don't know whether it will rain or not, but if it will, I shall stay at home.

6. There is no such a person here as you described just now.

7. Every time when I was in trouble, he would come to help me.

8. It will be 100 days since we take the College Entrance Examinations this year.

9. If or not it is fine, we will set off for the destination tomorrow morning.

10. The WTO cannot live up to its name while it does not include a country that is home to one fifth of mankind.

（三）语法填空

阅读下面材料，在空白处填入适当的内容（1个单词）或括号内单词的正确形式。

Mary will never forget the _____1_____（one）time she saw him. He suddenly appeared in class one day, _____2_____（wear）sunglasses. He walked in as if he _____3_____（buy）the school. And the word quickly got around that he was from New York City.

For some reason he sat beside Mary. Mary felt pleased, _____4_____ there were many empty seats in the room. But she quickly realized that it wasn't her, it was probably the fact that she sat in _____5_____ last row.

_____6_____ he thought he could escape attention by sitting at the back, he was wrong. It might have made it a little _____7_____（hard）for everyone because it meant they had to turn around, but that didn't stop the kids in the class. Of course whenever they turned to look at him, they had to look at Mary, ___8___ made her feel like a star.

"Do you need those glasses for medical reasons? " the teacher asked. The new boy shook his head. "Then I'd appreciate it ___9___ you didn't wear them in class. I like to look at your eyes when I'm speaking to you. " The new boy looked at the teacher for a few seconds and all the other students wondered ___10___ the boy would do. Then he took them off, gave a big smile and said, "That's cool."

（四）短文改错

Smartphone apps certainly make our life easier. Currently, it looks even if they can even help us with our homework. A wide various of study aid apps aimed at students have been released. Most of these apps allow users to take a photo of our schoolwork and the correct answers will just appear on their smartphones. Convenient although they are, these apps bring problems with both parents and teachers. Most students just copy the answers from the apps, when only a few use the apps to study. Better still, some students even use the study aid apps as social networks. Therefore, we are not making the suggestion that study aid apps should be banned. Parents and teachers should give necessary guidance to help students to take the advantage of the study aid apps' strengths and avoiding their weaknesses.

第十三章　定语从句

定语从句是中学生学习的重点语法之一。定语从句也叫作形容词性从句，在主从复合句中作定语的一个句子就是定语从句，要学好定语从句，就必须明确下面所讲的一些概念和区别。

一、明确关系代词与关系副词的作用

常用的关系代词有who，whom，whose，that，which，as，常用的关系副词有when，where，why等。关系词的作用有三：一是引导定语从句，二是代替先行词，三是在定语从句中作成分。

（1）who 指人，在定语从句中作主语。例如：

The pretty lady **who** spoke to you just now in the street is my English teacher.

刚才在街上跟你说话的那位漂亮女士是我的英语老师。

（2）whom指人，在定语从句中作宾语，可省略也可被that / who代替。例如：

The old man（**whom**）you met the other day in the supermarket is one of my close friends.

那天你在超市遇见的那位老人是我的一位好朋友。

（3）whose 可指人也可指物，表所属关系，在从句中作定语，相当于of whom，of which。例如：

The girl **whose** pronunciation is the best in your class is my daughter.

= The girl **of whom** the pronunciation is the best in your class is my daughter.

你们班发音最好的那个女孩是我女儿。

The new building **whose** color is mainly red was built last year.

= The new building **of which** the color is mainly red was built last year.

主体颜色是红色的那栋楼是去年修建的。

The boss, in **whose** company my mother is working, can speak English as well as Chinese.

那个老板除了会讲汉语还会讲英语，我妈妈在他的公司里上班。

（4）that既可指人也可指物，在定语从句中作主语、宾语和表语，作宾语和表语时可以省略。例如：

Yesterday I bought a novel **that** was written by a middle school student.（作主语）

昨天我买了一本中学生写的小说。

The people（**that**）you saved in the terrible earthquake are living happily now.（作宾语，可省略）

你在那次大地震中救出的人现在生活得很幸福。

China is no longer the country（**that**）it used to be thirty years ago.（作表语，可省略）

中国不再是三十年前的样子了。

（5）which 指物，在定语从句中作主语或宾语，作宾语时可以省略。例如：

This is a game **which** is very popular with children, especially, primary school students.（作主语）

这是一个受孩子们喜欢的游戏，尤其是小学生。

The picture（**which**）the teacher is drawing now is either like a cat or like a dog.（作宾语，可省略）

老师正在画的那幅画既像猫又像狗。

（6）as可以指人也可以指物，在定语从句中作主语或者宾语，通常有such, the same, so, as修饰先行词。例如：

He is **such a person as** nobody can usually understand.（作宾语）

他是那种通常没人能理解的人。

It is **so interesting a book as** is popular with both adults and children.（作主语）

这是大人小孩都喜欢的、如此有趣的一本书。

Believe it or not，this is **such an exciting film as** I have never seen.（作宾语）

信不信由你，这是我看过的如此令人兴奋的一部电影。

（7）when 表时间，在定语从句中作状语。例如：

They brought the hours back to me **when** I was taken good care of in that faraway village.

他们让我回想起我在那遥远的村庄被好好照顾的时光。

（8）where 表地点，在定语从句中作状语。例如：

Finally we came to a place **where** there were a lot of trees and flowers.

最终我们来到了有很多树和花的地方。

（9）why 表原因，在定语从句中作状语。例如：

Can you tell me the reason **why** you didn't come to the meeting yesterday?

你能告诉我你昨天没来开会的原因吗？

二、明确that与which的区别

1. 下列情况下只用that

（1）先行词为不定代词something，anything，nothing，everything，all，much，little，few，none等以及先行词被all，any，much，every，some，no，little，few等所修饰时。例如：

I'd like to know **everything that** she did when she was in New York，in the USA.

我想知道她在美国纽约做过的一切。

All the essays that were written by him were based on his practical teaching.

他写的所有论文都是以他的教学实践为基础的。

（2）先行词被形容词最高级修饰时。例如：

This is **the tallest** building **that** I've ever seen in my life.

这是我有生以来见过的最高的楼。

（3）先行词被序数词修饰时。例如：

This is **the first** English **film** that has been shown in our village.

这是我们村子里放映过的第一部英文电影。

（4）先行词中既有人又有物或动物时。例如：

Then we talked about the **persons and things that** we could remember in the school.

然后我们谈论起了能记得起的上学时的人和事。

（5）先行词被the only，the same，the very，the last 修饰时，但the same...that 表示"同一个……"，而the same...as 表示"相同的两个……"。例如：

This is **the very** dictionary **that** I'm looking for.

这正是我所找的字典。

This is **the same** taxi **that** I took yesterday.（同一辆车）

这就是我昨天坐的那辆出租车。

I'm going to buy **the same** dictionary **as** you have.（相同的两本字典）

我打算买和你的一样的字典。

（6）用在疑问代词who，which 开头的疑问句中。例如：

Who is the man **that** is standing over there and talking?

站在那边说话的那个人是谁？

Which is the blouse **that** you like most in the shopping window?

商店橱窗里你最喜欢的衬衫是哪件？

（7）关系代词在定语从句中作表语时多用that。例如：

The village is no longer the one **that** it used to be.（that作句末be的表语）

这个村子不再是过去的样子。

2. 下列情况下只用which

（1）非限制性定语从句中：

We usually have more vegetables rather than meat for supper, **which** I think is better for health.

我们晚饭通常宁愿吃蔬菜也不愿吃肉，我认为这样更有利于健康。

（2）介词+which：

We came to a farmhouse, **in front of which** sat a small boy.

我们来到了一个农舍，农舍前面坐着一个小男孩。

三、明确其他用法及区别

1. 用关系副词when，where，why还是关系代词which（that）

（1）当先行词是表示时间、地点及原因的名词时，关系词取决于先行词与从句中谓语动词的关系，如果先行词与从句中的动词是逻辑上的动宾关系或主谓关系，就用which或that作宾语或主语。例如：

I'll never forget the days **which**（**that**）we **spent** together during those hard times.（作从句中spent的宾语）

我永远都不会忘记我们在艰苦岁月里一起度过的那些日子。

I'll never forget the days **which**（**that**）**made** me strong and confident.（作定语从句中的主语）

我永远不会忘记那些使我变得坚强和自信的日子。

This is exactly the factory **which**（**that**）we **visited** ten years ago.（作visited的宾语）

这恰是十年前我们参观过的那家工厂。

This is exactly the factory **which**（**that**）**produced** leather shoes ten years ago.（作从句的主语）

这恰是十年前生产皮鞋的那家工厂。

That's the reason **which**（**that**）the boss **explained** at the meeting last week.（作explained的宾语）

那就是老板在上周会上解释的原因。

That's the reason **which**（**that**）**made** him leave the company last week.（作从句的主语）

那就是上周使他离开公司的理由。

（2）如果关系词在从句中作时间、地点、原因状语时分别用when，where，why，也可用介词+which来表达。例如：

I'll never forget the day **when**（=on which）I joined the Communist Party of China.（I joined the Communist Party of China **on the day=on which=when.**）

我永远都不会忘记我加入中国共产党的那一天。

This is the school where（= in which）we studied Spanish five years ago.（We studied Spanish five years ago **in the school=in which=where.**）

这就是五年前我们学习西班牙语的学校。

This is the factory where（= in which）we visited the advanced shop last year.（We visited the advanced shop **in the factory=in which=where.** 从句中visited 的宾语是the advanced shop）

这就是我们去年参观的那个先进车间的工厂。

The reason why（for which）I was late for the meeting was that I didn't catch the first bus.（I was late for the meeting **for the reason that...=for which=why.**）

我开会迟到的原因是没有赶上第一班公共汽车。

（3）如果有表地点的抽象名词，如：position，stage，point，case，situation，condition，scene，example，instance，activity，project，job，contest，sport等作先行词，定语从句中需要关系副词作地点状语时，也用where或者"介词+which"引导定语从句，但occasion后要用when或"介词+which"引导定语从句。例如：

Spelling Bee is a contest where（in which）competitors，usually children，are asked to spell as many words as possible.（Competitors，usually children，are asked to spell as many words as possible **in the contest=in which=where.**）

拼字游戏是一种比赛，比赛中参赛者，尤其是孩子，被要求拼出尽可能多的单词。

He has reached the point where（at which）he should change his attitude towards the job.（He should change his attitude towards the job **at this point=at which=where.**）

他已经到了应该改变工作态度的这个点了。

There are such occasions when（at which）students know a lot of words but can't write a good composition.（Students know a lot of words but can't write a good composition **at these occasions=at which=when.** occasion表时间，我们倒过来理解一下，occasionally 的意思是"偶尔"）

在这些时候，学生知道了很多单词，但不能写出一篇好作文。

2. which/as引导非限制性定语从句

有时候都可以指整个句子。但若表示主句和从句之间是"因果关系"时用which，而表示"正如……那样"且能放置句首时用as，除此以外可以换用。

He was late for his work again and again, **which** made the boss angry.（迟到导致生气）

他一次次地上班迟到，这使老板很生气。

As everybody can see, the elephant is more like a snake than anything else.

正如每个人所看到的那样，大象与其说像别的任何东西倒不如说像条蛇。

She married me at that time, which（as）was quite natural.（只简单指代前面这件事情时可换用）

她当时嫁给了我，这件事很自然。

3. 介词+which/ whom中介词从何而来

一般来讲，这个"介词"有四个来源。

（1）跟先行词的搭配有关：

I don't like the way **in** which you treat your husband.（in this way）

我不喜欢你对待你丈夫的那种方式。

（2）跟从句中动词或形容词搭配有关：

There was no one in the street **to** whom I could turn for help at that time.（turn to sb.）

街上当时没有我可以求助的人。

（3）表达"部分与整体的关系"或所属关系：

I have many dictionaries, one **of** which（of which one）is written in English.

我有很多本字典，其中一本是用英语写的。

She showed the visitors around the building, **of** which the repair work has taken more than two years.（of which the repair work = the repair work of which = whose repair work）

她带游客参观了那个建筑，那个建筑花了两年多时间被修复。

（4）与句意相一致：

They finally came to a farmhouse, in front of / behind / beside **which** stood a handsome boy.

他们最终来到了一个农舍，农舍前面/后面/旁边站着一个帅气的男孩。

（5）介词有时候也可加where，when：

She climbed up the top of the mountain, **from** where she could see some enemies in the distance.（from where = from **on** the top of the temple）

她爬到了山顶上，从那儿看到了远处的敌人。

He hid himself behind the door, **from** where he could give his friend a fright.（from where=from behind the door）

他藏在门背后，从那儿可以给他朋友一个惊吓。

She began to learn Spanish five years ago, **since** when she has always been occupied in it.（since when=since five years ago）

她五年前开始学西班牙语，自那时候起她一直忙于学习。

4. 定语从句中的主谓一致问题

当关系代词在从句中作主语时，谓语动词要跟先行词保持一致。例如：

I, who **am** a teacher, like teaching very much.

我是老师，我非常喜欢教书。

He, who **is** a teacher, likes teaching very much.

他是老师，他非常喜欢教书。

You, who **are** a teacher, like teaching very much.

你是老师，你非常喜欢教书。

He is one of the students who **have** passed the exams.（先行词是 students）

他是通过考试的学生之一。

He is **the only one** of the students who **has** failed in the exams.（先行词是 the only one）

他是学生中唯一没通过考试的人。

5. 定语从句和同位语从句的区别

定语从句和同位语从句的区别有三：其一，that引导定语从句时，在句中作主语、宾语或表语，作宾语和表语时可以省略，而that引导同位语从句时无词义、不作句子成分但不能省略；其二，定语从句是对先行词进行修饰限制或说明，而同位语从句是对其前面的名词所表达的具体内容的陈述；其三，定语从句中，that之前的内容不能省略，that可以被which代替；而同位语从句中，that之前的内容省略或改写后句子仍成立。例如：

The news **that** we got from the newspaper is true.（定语从句）

我们从报纸上得到的消息是真的。

The news **that** our basketball team has won the game is true.（同位语从句）

我们篮球队赢了比赛，这个消息是真的。

改写句1：**That** our basketball team has won the game is true.

改写句2：The news is **that** our basketball team has won the game.

6. where引导的定语从句和状语从句的区别

定语从句前面有表地点的名词作先行词，此时where可被in which 代替，而状语从句前面没有先行词，此时的where不能被in which代替，翻译并比较：树可以种在有足够雨水的地方。例如：

Trees can be planted in the **places where** （in which）there is enough water.（定语从句）

Trees can be planted **where** there is enough water.（状语从句）

再比较：他喜欢待在可以过一个幸福有趣的生活的城市。

He likes to stay in a **city where** （in which）he can live a happy and interesting life.

He likes to stay **where** he can live a happy and interesting life.

7. as引导的定语从句和结果状语从句的区别

定语从句中先行词被such，the same，as，so修饰时，关系代词用as且在定语从句中作主语或宾语。而要表达"如此……以至于……"时用that引导结果状语从句，但that句中不作成分。例如：

This is **such** a difficult problem **as** nobody can solve.（定语从句，as 作solve 的宾语，指problem）

这是如此难的没人能解决的一个问题。

This is **so** difficult a question that nobody can answer **it**.（状语从句中句子结构完整）

这是如此难的一个问题，以至于没人能回答上来。

8. 限制性定语从句和非限制性定语从句的区别

限制性定语从句和非限制性定语从句的区别。例如：

Her brother who is now working in Beijing often encourages her to go to college.

她在北京工作的哥哥经常鼓励她要上大学。（不止一个哥哥）

Her brother，who is now working in Beijing，often encourages her to go to college.

她哥哥经常鼓励她要上大学，他现在在北京工作。（只有一个哥哥）

when，where 也可以引导非限制性定语从句，但why 一般不引导非限制性定语从句。例如：

She arrived at the meeting room at 9 o'clock，**when** all the people were seated for the meeting.

她9点到了会议室，那时所有的人已经坐好等待开会。

Finally we came to a town，**where** all the people were busy doing their business.

最后我们来到了一座小城，那儿所有的人都忙着自己的事业。

Can you tell me the reason **why** you don't like English?

你能告诉我你不喜欢英语的原因吗？

9. that用作关系副词的情况

当先行词是表示时间、地点、原因、方式的名词the time，the place，the reason，the way时，that 代替when，where，why，in / by which引导定语从句，也可以省略。例如：

This is the first time （**that**） we have experienced such a terrible earthquake. （注意时态：主句一般现在时，从句现在完成时）

这是我们第一次经历如此可怕的地震。

It was the second time （**that**） he had been invited to such a formal occasion. （注意时态：主句一般过去时，从句过去完成时）

这是他第二次被邀请到如此正式的场合。

He is unlikely to find the place （**that**） he lived with his parents forty years ago.

他不可能找到四十年前和父母一起生活过的地方。

The reason （**that**） she was late for the appointment was probably that she wanted to test him.

她约会迟到的原因有可能是想考验他。

I don't like the way （**that / in which**） you treat your father-in-law.

我不喜欢你对待岳父大人的那种方式。

Exercise Thirteen

（一）单句语法填空

1. I have many friends, _____ some are rich and successful businessmen.

2. I work in a business _____ almost everyone is waiting for a great chance.

3. _____ is often the case, we have worked out the production plan ahead of time.

4. On the bus I saw a girl _____ I thought was your daughter.

5. Can you think of a case _____ you are mistaken by others, but you can't tell the truth?

6. I don't like the way _____ you speak to her.

7. When people talk about the cities of the US, the first _____ comes into their mind is New York.

8. The reason _____ she was late for school was _____ she had been knocked down.

9. You must show my wife the same respect _____ you show me.

10. Who is the man _____ is sweeping the floor over there?

（二）单句改错

1. This is the museum where I once visited five years ago.

2. The pencil with that he is writing was sent by his sister.

3. This is the house which I bought it in 2019 before I got married.

4. The first English book which I read was *Gone with the Wind*.

5. All what we saw there was very interesting and inspiring.

6. The child who parents went to help in hospitals in Wuhan is called Li Liang.

7. He is the only one of the students who have an expensive car in this class.

8. There are occasions where students know a lot of words but can't write a good composition.

9. They produced 100 thousand cars last year, most of them were sold abroad.

10. Is there any restaurant around which we can eat something?

（三）语法填空

阅读下面材料，在空白处填入适当的内容（1个单词）或括号内单词的正确形式。

Hello, everyone! This is the first time ___1___ I ___2___ (be) here. Now please allow me to introduce my school and my class. OK. I'm an English teacher from the best high school ___3___ is located in the east of Lanzhou. There are 45 students in my class, ___4___ parents are all farmers. My class number is three, of ___5___ the name is Pearl Class. It is a good class ___6___ every student studies very hard. Li Hua, ___7___ was elected by her classmates at the beginning of the term, is monitor of the class. She is a friendly student ___8___ her classmates like and trust very much. And she is one of the students who ___9___ (be) interested in and good at English but Jin Long is the only one of them who ___10___ (have) an iPhone 13 in the class.

（四）短文改错

In order to leave some impressive memories for both of us before graduation, our class made a special video express our appreciation to our school. Firstly, we carried out a discussion about how to design a video. During the discussion, various detail were put forward. Secondly, we began to make the video. We not only shot some wonderful videos in the school yard and interviewed our teachers, which expressed best wishes for us. Finally, those that are good at computers contribute to clipping the video. The show received a warm welcome between our fellow schoolmates. When they saw the video, moments of the past flooded into our minds.

第十四章　名词性从句

名词性从句也是高中英语语法学习中的一个难点和热点。名词性从句包括主语从句、宾语从句、表语从句以及同位语从句。引导名词性从句的连接词有三类。

（1）连接词that：没有词义；不作句子成分；在部分宾语从句中可以省略，其他名词性从句中不能省略。

（2）连接词whether / if：词义"是否"；不作句子成分，不能省略；在部分宾语从句中whether 和 if可以互换，其他名词性从句中只用whether。

（3）连接代词what，whatever，which，whichever，who，whoever，whom，whomever，whose 以及连接副词when，whenever，where，wherever，how，however，why等，有词义；在从句中作主语、宾语、表语及状语，不能省略。

一、主语从句

（1）在一个主从复合句中由一个句子来充当主语，这个句子就叫作主语从句。例如：

That he is the best student in the class is obvious.

很明显，他是班上最好的学生。

Whether she will come to the meeting has not been known yet.

她是否来开会还不知道。

How the visitors will come depends on themselves.

那些参观者怎么来取决于他们自己。

（2）当名词性从句作主语时，主句谓语动词通常用单数，即大多数主语从句后用单数动词，但what引导的主语从句中谓语动词是need，want等的时候，主句谓语动词有时和表语保持一致。例如：

What I am most interested in **is** American movies.

我非常感兴趣的是美国电影。

What I need **is** a large amount of money.

我所需要的是一大笔钱。

What I need **are** a great many books.

我所需要的是大量的书。

（3）为了避免头重脚轻，在英语中经常用it作形式主语， 而把主语从句放在后面作真正主语，通常有以下四种句式：

第一，It + be + 形容词 + that-从句。例如：

It is obvious that English is becoming more and more popular all over the world.

很明显英语在全世界越来越流行。

It is necessary that everybody should read English aloud for at least 20 minutes every morning.

每人每天早晨至少大声朗读20分钟英语是必要的。

第二，It + be + 过去分词 + that-从句。

It is well-known to us **that** the earth is round and travels around the sun.

众所周知，地球是圆的并且绕着太阳转。

It is believed that China will become the most powerful country in the world.

大家认为，中国将成为世界上最强大的国家。

第三，It + be + 名词 + that-从句。

It is a pity that such a hard-working student didn't pass the examination.

真可惜，如此勤奋的一名学生没通过考试。

It is no wonder that she was crying after class this morning.

难怪她今天早晨下课后哭呢。

第四，It + 不及物动词 + that-从句。

It happens that I don't have much money on me today.

今天碰巧我身上也没多带钱。

It occurred to me that I had left my wallet in that restaurant.

我突然想起我把皮夹落在那个饭馆了。

（4）其他含有it作形式主语的句型：

It makes no difference where we will spend our holidays.

我们在哪里度假没什么区别。

It doesn't matter whether he will come to the meeting or not.

他来不来开会都不要紧。

It remains to be seen whether the old couple will go abroad for their holiday.

这老两口是否去国外度假还有待验证。

二、宾语从句

1. 宾语从句的定义

在一个主从复合句中由一个句子来充当宾语，这个句子就叫作宾语从句。宾语从句可以是及物动词的宾语，也可以是介词的宾语。

John said that he was leaving for London on Wednesday.

约翰说他星期三动身去伦敦。

She told me that she would accept my invitation.

她告诉我她会接受我的邀请。

I worry about whether he can get over the illness.

我担忧他能否克服疾病。

The teacher doesn't know who broke the window carelessly before class.

老师不知道谁在课前不小心打破了窗户。

I will do whatever the people think necessary and important.

我会去做人们认为一切必要和重要的事。

Our success depends upon how well we can cooperate with one another.

我们的成功依赖于我们相互合作的程度。

2. 用it作形式宾语

用it作形式宾语，把宾语从句放在后面作真正宾语，常见句式有：

（1）主语+动词+it+形容词或名词+that-从句，常用动词有make，think，consider，feel，find 等。例如：

He thinks it necessary that students should take down some notes in English classes.

他认为学生们在英语课堂上记笔记是必要的。

We have made it a rule that we don't watch TV while we have meals.

我们把吃饭时不看电视定为一个规矩。

（2）主语+动词+it+从句，常用动词和短语有like，love，enjoy，appreciate，hate，dislike，see to，rely on，depend on，count on等。例如：

I hate it when people speak with their mouths full of food.

我讨厌人们用装满食物的嘴说话。

I appreciate it if you listen to me attentively in class and revise what we learn in time after class.

你如果课堂上认真听讲，下课后及时复习所学内容的话，我非常欣赏。

You may depend on it that we shall never forget what you have said to us forever.

你可以放心，我们永远不会忘记你所说的话。

I will see to it that each child shall be given two eggs every day for the sake of health.

为了健康，每个孩子每天都必须得到两个鸡蛋，这事由我负责。

3. 引导宾语从句的that经常可以省略，但在下列情况下不省略

（1）在由and，or 连接的第二个及往后的宾语从句中，例如：

He thought（that）everybody should be treated equally and that they should be well educated.

他认为每个人应该被公平对待，他们应该接受良好教育。

（2）宾语从句作介词宾语时，例如：

I know nothing about her except / but that she likes singing and dancing.

对她，我一无所知，只知道她喜欢唱歌跳舞。

（3）当谓语动词与that从句中有插入语时，如：

They decided，in view of her perfect performance，that she was employed immediately.

由于她完美的表现，他们觉得她应该被立即录用。

4. 宾语从句中whether和if会常常换用，但在下列情况下只用whether

（1）宾语从句前置时，例如：

Whether he will come to help us，I don't know.

他来不来帮我们，我不知道。

（2）宾语从句作介词宾语时，例如：

I haven't solved the problem of whether I will go abroad for further study.

我还没解决我是否去国外深造的问题。

（3）与or not 连用时，例如：

I don't know whether or not I will be given a chance to speak at the meeting.

我不知道我是否被给一个机会在会上发言。

（4）后跟动词不定式时，例如：

We can't decide whether to accept his invitation.

我们还不能决定是否该接受他的邀请。

5. 宾语从句中的否定转移及反意疑问句

当主句中的谓语动词是think，believe，suppose，expect，guess，imagine等时，宾语从句中的否定转移到主句中来。当主句的主语是第一人称，其反意疑问句与宾语从句保持一致；当主句的主语为第二、三人称，其反意疑问句与主句保持一致；因为前面有否定形式，故反意疑问句中用肯定形式。例如：

I don't think that she can pass the driving test without practice，can she?

我认为她不训练是不能通过驾驶测试的，是吗?

They don't believe that he will treat his students in that way，do they?

他们不相信他会那样对待自己的学生，是吗?

6. 宾语从句中的时态问题

当主句的谓语为一般现在时或一般将来时时，宾语从句的谓语动词可以用所需要的任何时态；当主句谓语为一般过去时，宾语从句动词经常用相应的某种过去时态，但如果从句叙述的是客观真理或自然现象，可以用一般现在时或所需任何时态。例如：

I think that Mary has been well educated and she did very well in the interview yesterday.

我认为玛丽接受了良好的教育，并且在昨天的面试中表现得很好。

I **knew** that Johnson **had finished** his task and **would have** a long rest.

我知道约翰逊已经完成了自己的任务，并且要长时间休息。

The teacher **said** that the earth **is** round but not smooth.

老师说，地球是圆的但表面不光滑。

三、表语从句

（1）在一个主从复合句中由一个句子充当表语，这个句子叫作表语从句。表语从句通常放在系动词be，look，seem 等之后，除上面提到的连接词以外还可以用as if / as though引导，但as if / as though引导的从句若表示与事实相反或实现的可能性较小时，表语从句的谓语动词要用虚拟语气。例如：

The reason why he didn't tell you the truth was **that** he didn't want to make you unhappy.（此处不能用because，因为the reason作句子主语）

他没有告诉你真相的原因是他不想让你不快乐。

The problem is **whether** my parents will allow me to go to work in Tibet.

问题是我的父母会不会允许我去西藏工作。

He was no longer **what** he used to be ten years ago.

他不再是十年前的样子。

When a pencil is partly in a glass of water，it looks as if it **were** broken.（与事实相反，故用虚拟语气）

当一支铅笔的部分被放进水中时，它看起来好像折了。

It looks as though it **is going to rain** soon.（接近事实，故不用虚拟语气）

天看起来马上就要下雨了。

（2）because 和why都可以引导表语从句，但because 引导的表语从句表示原因，why 引导的表语从句表示结果。例如：

—I drove to Shanghai for an important conference yesterday.

我昨天开车去上海开一个重要大会了。

—Is that **why** you didn't come to the office? （结果是：没来办公室）

那就是你没来办公室的原因吗？

—**Why** didn't you come to the office yesterday?

昨天你为什么没来办公室？

—That's **because** I drove to Shanghai for an important conference. （说明没来办公室的原因）

那是因为我开车去上海开一个重要大会了。

四、同位语从句

在主从复合句中用来说明前面某个名词所表达的具体内容的一个句子就叫作同位语从句。同位语从句一般放在这些名词之后：fact，news，idea，hope，wish，promise，truth，suggestion，thought，question，doubt，conclusion，belief，order，word，possibility，chance，explanation，problem等。

Despite the **fact** that he doesn't like English，he has to study it hard.

尽管他不喜欢英语是事实，但他不得不努力学习。

I have no **idea** whether he will visit me at Christmas.

我不知道圣诞节期间他是否来看我。

I have no **idea** at all why more and more students are losing interest in English.

我一点都不知道为什么越来越多的学生对英语失去兴趣。

五、名词性从句的难点

（1）what引导名词性从句时可从以下三个维度去理解：what 在从句中要充当主语、宾语或表语，what 经常译为"所……的东西"，what=the thing（s）that。例如：

What made the school proud was that more than 90% of the students had been admitted to key universities.（what作主语从句中的主语）

使学校感到自豪的事情是90%以上的学生被重点大学录取。

What the students want to do is to continue their studies abroad after graduation.（what作主语从句中的宾语）

学生们想做的事情是毕业以后去国外深造。

The country is no longer **what** it used to be thirty years ago.（what 作表语从句中的表语）

这个国家不再是三十年以前的样子了。

（2）wh+ever与no matter+wh-的用法。引导让步状语从句时可以换用，引导名词性从句时只能用wh+ever。例如：

Wherever you go and whatever you do，I'll be right here waiting for you.

=**No matter where** you go and no matter what you do，I'll be right here waiting for you.

无论你去哪儿，无论你做什么，我都在这儿等着你。

Whatever you said at the meeting is worth thinking and using for reference.（主语从句，不能替换）

你在会上所说的一切都值得思考和借鉴。

Whoever is in the office，please give the note to him.

=**No matter who** is in the office，please give the note to him.

谁在办公室就把便条给他。

Please give the note to **whoever** is in the office.（宾语从句，不能替换）

请把便条给在办公室的任何人。

（3）名词性从句中的语序问题。名词性从句中统统要用陈述句语序，即主语在前，谓语在后。例如：

Where **he will go** to spend his holiday has not been known yet.

他将去哪里度假还不知道。

Can you tell me what **he did** in the English class yesterday?

你能告诉我他昨天在英语课堂上做什么了吗?

The problem is why **all the fish have died** out in the pond.

问题是池塘里的鱼为什么死光了。

Nobody can explain the mystery why **she suddenly disappeared**.

没人能解开她突然消失这个谜。

但翻译"我不知道他怎么了"时要**注意**：

I didn't know what the matter was with him.（错误）

I didn't know what was the matter with him.（正确，what是主语，the matter=wrong，是表语）

（4）表示"建议""要求""命令""主张"等意义的动词有suggest, advise, recommend, ask, require, request, demand, desire, order, command, insist, urge 以及它们的名词suggestion, advice, requirement, request, order等出现在主句中时，相关的名词性从句中用should + 动词原形，should可省略，如翻译：

他们建议把那些年轻小伙子派到西藏去工作。

It was suggested that those young men **should be sent** to work in Tibet.（主语从句）

They suggested that those young men **should be sent** to work in Tibet.（宾语从句）

Their suggestion was that those young men **should be sent** to work in Tibet.（表语从句）

They put forward the suggestion that those young men **should be sent** to work in Tibet.（同位语从句）

Exercise Fourteen

（一）单句语法填空

1. It is uncertain _____ side effect the medicine will bring about, although about two thousand patients have taken it.

2. One reason for her preference for city life is _____ she can have easy access to places like shops and restaurants.

3. The mother didn't know _____ to blame for the broken glass as it happened while she was out.

4. Our hometown is quite different from _____ it was before.

5. There is clear evidence _____ the most difficult feeling of all to interpret is bodily pain.

6. _____ we will go camping tomorrow depends on the weather.

7. Scientists are studying _____ human brains work to make computers.

8. The reason _____ he was late for school was _____ he had to send his mother to a hospital.

9. _____ leaves the room last ought to turn off the lights.

10. We don't doubt _____ he can do a good job.

（二）单句改错

1. What she was chosen as president of the company made us very happy.

2. That we need most at the moment is more time rather than money or anything else.

3. When you are there, please give the letter to whomever is in the office.

4. Whom will go to attend the meeting is extremely important.

5. We heard the news our women volleyball team had won the match.

6. You have no idea that how worried I was at that moment when my dog was lost!

7. I don't doubt whether the good news is true.

8. The reason why I have to go is because she will be disappointed if I don't.

9. My suggestion is that the young man will be sent to work in Tibet.

10. Since you have seen both fighters, who you think will win?

（三）语法填空

阅读下面材料，在空白处填入适当的内容（1个单词）或括号内单词的正确形式。

In some schools of America, most teachers say they are required to teach handwriting. But one of the studies found ___1___ about three fourths teachers say they are not prepared to teach handwriting. Many experts also think handwriting shouldn't be taught by itself. Instead, they say it should be used as an approach to ___2___ （get） students to express ideas.

In China, teachers ___3___ （common） report that one fourth students have poor handwriting. Some people might think handwriting is not important any more because ___4___ computers and voice recognition programs. Recently, some schools have offered handwriting lessons to their students, which has led to a ___5___ （heat） debate among people. Some people hold the opinion ___6___ the schools need handwriting lessons. For one thing, the traditional Chinese handwriting does not lose its charm but attracts many foreigners. So handwriting has become ___7___ important medium of cultural communication between China and other countries. For another, learning handwriting is of essential ___8___ （important） to youngsters, and the practice of handwriting can help develop many capabilities, such as the capability of concentrating and learning. Other people, however, tend to believe ____9____ it is useless for the students to learn handwriting at all. ____10____ the students need to do is having a good knowledge of computer programs. Since almost all documents are typed, we only need to learn typing.

（四）短文改错

This morning, our art teacher delivered to us a interesting lecture about Chinese paper-cut art. Entered the classroom, she was given a warm welcome. First of all, she told us what Chinese paper-cut is a traditional art form and it's a kind of folk culture with a long history. Then, she shows us the basic steps and skills of paper-cut. All of us listened and watched careful. After that, I began to try under her directions. Guided patiently by our teacher, we all finished our own work on time, we were happy to have such a good time.

第十五章　句子结构

一、按照用途分

英语中的句子按照其用途分为陈述句、祈使句、疑问句和感叹句。

1. 陈述句

用来陈述或者说明一件事实的句子叫作陈述句。例如：

He didn't work hard, so he didn't finish his task on time.

他不努力工作，所以没有按时完成任务。

There are many beautiful green trees in the park near my home.

我家附近的公园里有很多漂亮的绿树。

He is a famous professor and he is well-known for his scientific research.

他是位著名教授并且以科研而著称。

2. 祈使句

（1）用来发出命令、请求等的句子叫作祈使句。祈使句的主语是you，通常都会省略。例如：

Read the text we learned yesterday as loudly as possible, please.

请把昨天学过的课文尽可能大声地朗读一下。

Don't travel alone if you cannot deal with some difficulties.（祈使句的否定句）

如果不能对付困难，就不要独自旅游。

Do come by six o'clock.（祈使句的强调句）

务必在六点以前回来。

（2）祈使句中表示"分配任务"等的时候一般不省略主语。例如：

Tom, you clean the window. Peter, you fetch water. John, you sweep the floor.

汤姆，你擦玻璃；皮特，你去打水；约翰，你扫地。

Someone open the door and the window! （要用动词原形）

谁把门窗开一下！

（3）肯定祈使句的反意疑问句用will you 或won't you，否定祈使句只用will you；let's包括说话者和听话者双方，故反意疑问句中用shall we表示征求意见，而let us只表示说话者一方，故用will you表示请求。例如：

Speak slowly, **will you / won't you**?

说慢点，好吗？

Don't sit in my seat, **will you**?

不要坐在我的座位上，好吗？

Let's go and have a swim this afternoon, **shall we**?

=**Shall we** go and have a swim this afternoon?

咱们下午去游泳，好吗？

Let us stop working and go home, **will you**?

=**Will you** let us stop working and go home?

让我们停止工作回家，好吗？

（4）祈使句+and / or+陈述句也是一种常用句型，这个陈述句中多用一般将来时。祈使句可以转化为条件状语从句，当然连接词and或者or要省略。例如：

Use your head **and** you will find the answer to the question.

=If you use your head, you will find the answer to the question.

仔细想想，你就会找到问题的答案。

One more word **and** you will have to go away.

=If you say one more word, you will have to go away.

你再多说一句就走人。

Hurry up **or** you will be late for the conference.

=If you don't hurry up, you will be late for the conference.

快点吧，否则你就会开会迟到的。

Work as hard as possible **or** you will fall behind others.

=If you don't work as hard as possible，you will fall behind others.

尽可能努力地工作，否则你又会落后于别人。

3. 疑问句

（1）疑问句就是提出问题的句子，包括一般疑问句、特殊疑问句、选择疑问句以及反意疑问句，疑问句中要用倒装语序。选择疑问句和特殊疑问句不能用yes和no来回答。例如：

—Are you a student from No. 1 Middle School of Lanzhou?

你是兰州一中的学生吗？

—Yes，I am. / No，I am not.

是的，我是。/ 不，我不是。

—Don't you work in the company?

你不在那家公司上班了吗？

—No，I don't. It's years since I worked there.

是的，不上了。我都几年不在那儿上班了。

—How long have you been in the army?

你在这个部队多久了？

—**For** three years.

三年了。

—How soon will you come back from America?

你多久才能从美国回来？

—**In** three years.

三年后。

—How often do you go to see your parents in the countryside?

你多久去乡下看父母一次？

—**Twice** a year.

一年两次。

—Are you a university student or a high school student?

你是大学生还是中学生？

—I'm a high school student.

我是中学生。

（2）反意疑问句由陈述句加疑问句构成，一般来说，前半部分是肯定，后半部分是否定，前半部分是否定，后半部分是肯定；疑问部分一定要用人称代词且与陈述句中的人称保持一致；疑问部分的助动词、系动词和情态动词也要与陈述句一致，如果是否定要缩写；回答时与汉语不同，只要事实肯定就用yes，事实否定就用no。例如：

They have a big square wooden house, **haven't** they / **don't** they? （have表"有"，可直接构成否定或疑问）

他们有一栋大方形木屋，是吗？

They seldom have lunch at home, **do** they? （have除表"有"以外的意思时要借助助动词构成否定或者疑问）

他们很少在家里吃午饭，是吗？

There will be a meeting tomorrow, **won't** there?

明天要开个会，是不是？

He ought to look after his grandparents well, **oughtn't** he?

他应该照顾好他的祖父母，是吗？

You'd better take an umbrella with you, **hadn't** you / **shouldn't** you?

你最好随身带把雨伞，好吗？

The nurse must take good care of the patients, **mustn't** she?

这名护士必须要照顾好这些病人，是吗？

You must buy a personal computer, **needn't** you?

你现在有必要买一台个人电脑吗？

（3）must表推测时，反意疑问句要依陈述事实来进行变化。例如：

He must be a teacher from our school, **isn't** he?

他一定是我们学校的老师，是不是？

It must have rained last night, **didn't** it?

昨晚天一定下雨了，是吗？

They must have lived here for at least 10 years so far, **haven't** they?

到目前为止他们在这儿住了至少有10年了，是吗？

They must have lived here for at least 10 years by the end of last year, **hadn't** they?

到去年为止他们在这儿住了至少有10年了，是吗？

（4）不定代词、动名词、动词不定式以及主语从句作主语时，请注意反意疑问句中所用代词：

Everyone here likes eating beef noodles, **don't** they / **doesn't** he?

这儿的每个人都喜欢吃牛肉面，是吗？

Nothing could make him against his country, **could** it?

什么都不能使他背叛自己的祖国，是吗？

Practising speaking English every day is what an English learner must do, **isn't** it?

练习每天说英语是学英语的人必须要做的事，是吗？

What he talked about in the lecture was very instructive, **wasn't** it?

他在报告中所谈论的内容非常有教育意义，是吗？

（5）主句主语为I 时，注意反意疑问句的否定式aren't；主句中出现want，wish等动词时，反意疑问句表示征求对方意见，故用may I。例如：

I am not wounded seriously, **am** I?

我伤得不重，是吧？

I am honest and loyal to you, **aren't** I?

我既诚实又忠于你，不是吗？

I want to go home for a rest, **may** I?

我想回家休息一会儿，可以吗？

I wish to be allowed to surf the Internet now, **may** I?

我现在想能被容许上会儿网，可以吗？

（6）当主句的谓语动词think，believe，suppose，guess，expect，imagine，be sure，be afraid等后跟一个宾语从句时，反意疑问句的变化规则是：如果主句主语为第一人称时，依宾语从句而变；如果主句主语是二、三人称时，依主句而变。例如：

I don't think that **he** is honest, is he?

我认为他不诚实，是吗？

They don't think that he is honest, do they?

他们不认为他诚实, 是吗?

（7）当谓语动词是上述动词以外的动词时或者其他的主从复合句, 反意疑问句一律依主句而变; 并列句的反意疑问句依最接近的一个单句而变。例如:

I told him that the meeting would be put off till next week, **didn't** I?

我告诉他会议推迟到下周了, 不是吗?

When she was young, she used to play the piano, **usedn't** she / **didn't** she?

她年轻时常常弹钢琴, 是吗?

She is a nurse but her husband isn't a doctor, **is he?**

她是护士而她丈夫不是医生, 是吗?

（8）当表示惊讶、关心、讽刺等感情色彩时, 主句用肯定形式, 反意疑问句用肯定形式; 主句用否定形式, 反意疑问句用否定形式, 表示说话者已经知道答案, 只是加以确认而已, 往往以so, then等副词开头。例如:

So you were not listening to me just now, **weren't** you?

这么说来你刚才没听我说话, 是吗?

Then you are a student from No. 1 Middle School, **are** you?

那你是一名第一中学的学生, 是吧?

4. 感叹句

感叹句是用来表达说话人的情感、态度以及对某事看法的句子, 通常以what和how开头, what用来修饰名词, 包括单数可数名词、名词复数以及不可数名词; how用来修饰形容词、副词等。例如:

What a beautiful flower it is!

多美丽的花呀!

What pretty girls they are!

她们是多美的女孩啊!

What fine weather it is today!

今天的天气多好啊!

How sweet the flower smells!

这花闻起来多香啊!

How fast the little girl runs!

这小女孩跑得好快啊!

How I wish I were ten years younger!

我多么希望自己年轻十岁!

二、按照结构分

按照结构来分,英语句子分为简单句、并列句和复合句三种。

1. 简单句

(1)简单句就是一个或多个主语共有一个或多个谓语。例如:

Tom, Johnson and Peter entered the room, turned on the light and sat on the sofa.

汤姆、约翰逊和皮特进了屋子、开了灯并坐在沙发上。

(2)常见简单句的五种基本结构:

第一,主语+谓语(S+V)。

She is laughing loudly and happily.

她在大声而快乐地笑。

第二,主语+谓语+宾语(S+V+O)。

We speak English in class every day.

我们每天在课堂上讲英语。

第三,主语+系动词+表语(S+Link-V+P)。

They are all Germans.

他们都是德国人。

第四,主语+谓语+直接宾语+间接宾语(S+V+DO+IO)。

He offered me some books yesterday.

昨天他主动给了我几本书。

第五,主语+谓语+宾语+宾补(S+V+O+C)。

Who left the door open?

谁没关门?(谁使门敞开着?)

2. 并列句

两个或两个以上的简单句由并列连词连起来就叫作并列句,常用的并列连词有:and,or,so,but,for,while,when,not only...but also...,either...or..., neither... nor..., etc。例如：

He was very tired **and** he went to bed early last night.

昨晚他很累并且早早就睡觉了。

Use your head **and** you will think out a good way to solve the problem.

仔细想想，你就会想出一个解决问题的好办法。

Hurry up **or** you will be late for the meeting again.

快点，否则你就会再次开会迟到的。

He had been told about it many times，**but** he made the same mistake.

告诉过他多次那件事，但他还是犯了同样的错误。

The day broke，**for** the birds were singing happily.（for表示补充理由）

天亮了，因为鸟在快乐地叫着。

He is very tall and strong **while** his wife is very short and weak.

他又高又壮，而他妻子又矮又弱。

She was walking in the street **when** a man came up and robbed her of her handbag.

她正在街上走着，这个时候一个男子走上来，抢了她的包。

Not only did he come to school early，**but also** his homework was finished ahead of time.

他不仅到校早，而且作业也提前完成。

Either she will give up her hope，**or** her parents will change their mind.

要么她放弃希望，要么她爸妈改变主意。

Neither do I know his address，**nor** does my husband.

我不知道他的地址，我丈夫也不知道。

3. 复合句

一个主句加一个或多个从句就叫作复合句，或主从复合句。通常含有状语从句、定语从句和名词性从句的句子就是复合句。例如：

If you laugh，the world laughs with you；**if** you cry，you cry alone.（含有状语从句的复合句）

你笑，大家跟你一起笑；你哭，你就独自哭吧。

The man **who** cannot reach the Great Wall is not a true man. （含有定语从句的复合句）

不到长城非好汉。

What he likes most is reading newspapers and surfing the Internet. （含有主语从句的复合句）

他最喜欢的是读报和上网。

Exercise Fifteen

（一）单句语法填空

1. We forgot to bring our tickets, but please let us enter, _____?

2. I'm sure you'd rather she went to school by bus, _____?

3. The artist was born poor, _____ poor he remained all his life.

4. In some places women are expected to earn money _____ men work at home and raise children.

5. Follow your doctor's advice, _____ your cough will get worse.

6. The day broke, _____ the birds were singing happily outside.

7. I had just stepped out of the bathroom and was busily drying myself with a towel _____ I heard the steps.

8. —English has a large vocabulary, hasn't it?

　　—Yes. _____ more words and expressions and you will find it easier to read and write.

9. _____ I wish I were twenty years younger!

10. He had been told about it many times, _____ he still made the same mistake.

（二）单句改错

1. I will surely let you know as soon as they will arrive here.

2. The young soldier was taken to the hospital because of he had been wounded seriously on the battlefield.

3. So far as I know, there are five people were killed in the accident.

4. How a lot of work here I have to finish today!

5. He must be a teacher from our school, mustn't he?

6. Hurry up and you will be late for the meeting again.

7. —How soon do you go to see your parents in the countryside?

　　—Twice a year.

8. What surprised me was not what he said but in the way he said it.

9. It's no use explain such things to the little child.

10. It was at eleven-thirty when he came back home from office.

（三）语法填空

阅读下面材料，在空白处填入适当的内容（1个单词）或括号内单词的正确形式。

Online shopping is coming into fashion in most cities, ___1___ people are able to make full use of the rapidly-developed Internet technology. Nowadays, can we find a person who hasn't experienced online shopping? Definitely not.

Online shopping ___2___ (welcome) by most people due to various reasons. From the perspective（视角）of the consumer, it can save some time for people who don't have much spare time. Just click the mouse, they can get ___3___ they want while staying at home. For the retailers（零售商）, it can cut some costs for those who don't have many circulating funds.

___4___ (compare) with the traditional trade mode（风格）, it saves them the need to rent a house. ___5___, there are still some ___6___ (advantage) in online shopping. First, a face-to-face deal makes online shopping less reliable and trustworthy. Second, people will lose the fun of bargain.

___7___ is undeniable（不可否认的）that shopping on the Internet has become an irresistible（无法抗拒的）trend in modern ___8___ (social). It's of great urgency that we need to make the relative laws with the rapid growth of online shopping. ___9___ in this way can we enjoy the pleasure and convenience of online shopping without the concern of ___10___ (cheat).

（四）短文改错

In most cases, the very first thing that we ask for when visit a cafe or friend's house is the WiFi password. It's almost unlike the Internet has become one of our basic needs. And according to technology Website Digital Trends, up to 60 percent of people in the world still didn't have an Internet connection. The situation is even more worse in the least developed countries—only one tenth of the people has regular access to the Internet. That's why in the recent survey in the US, 68 percent of the respondents think of Internet access to a privilege instead of a human right.

However, the United Nations made this clear in a report back in 2011 that it believes Internet access should be a human right and it "should be a priority（优先考虑的事）for all states" to make sure everyone has access to the web.

第十六章　特殊句式——强调、倒装及省略

一、强调句型

1. 强调句型的用法

当英语句子中的动词是一般现在时和一般过去时的时候，可以用do，第三人称用does和did对动词进行强调，其后的动词用原形。例如：

We **do like** Lanzhou beef noodles.

我们确实喜欢兰州牛肉面。

She **does get up** early every morning in order to read English aloud.

她为了朗读英语真的每天早上起得很早。

He **did come** to help us when we were in trouble.

在我们处于麻烦中的时候，他真的来帮我们了。

Do come to the meeting tomorrow please；it's very urgent.

明天请务必来开会，很要紧的。

2. 区分强调句型及强调句型范例

其他句子成分可以放在It is（was）...that / who（指人）句式中进行强调，但表语、比较状语、让步状语以及since，as引导的原因状语一般不被强调。要判断是否是强调句式时，把it is...that 去掉，句子结构仍然成立、意思完整，那就是强调句型了；属于现在范畴的时态用it is来强调，属于过去范畴的时态用it was来强调。强调句有陈述句、一般疑问句以及特殊疑问句等形式，还可以转化为宾语从句，以下面的句子为例分别对主语、宾语、地点状语和时间状语进行强调。

He played basketball on the playground yesterday.

（1）陈述的强调句型：

It was **he** that / who played basketball on the playground yesterday.

It was **basketball** that he played on the playground yesterday.

It was **on the playground** that he played basketball yesterday.

It was **yesterday** that he played basketball on the playground.

（2）一般疑问的强调句型：

Was it **he** that / who played basketball on the playground yesterday?

Was it **basketball** that he played on the playground yesterday?

Was it **on the playground** that he played basketball yesterday?

Was it **yesterday** that he played basketball on the playground?

（3）特殊疑问的强调句型：

Who was it that / who played basketball on the playground yesterday?

What was it that he played on the playground yesterday?

Where was it that he played basketball yesterday?

When was it that he played basketball on the playground?

（4）转化为宾语从句的强调句型：

Can you tell me **who** it was that played basketball on the playground yesterday?

Can you tell me **what** it was that he played on the playground yesterday?

Can you tell me **where** it was that he played basketball yesterday?

Can you tell me **when** it was that he played basketball on the playground?

3. 强调句型与其他it开头的句式的区别

强调句型中的It is...that去掉后句意不受影响，而其他句式则不然。例如：

It was **at eight** o'clock that visitors finally arrived at the hotel.（强调句型）

=At eight o'clock visitors finally arrived at the hotel.（去掉It was...that后句意完整）

参观者最终是八点钟到达宾馆的。

It was **eight** o'clock when visitors finally arrived at the hotel.（it表时间，when引导状语从句。去掉it was...后句意不完整）

当参观者到达宾馆时，时间是八点钟。

It is time that we got up and went to school.（it表时间，that引导定语从句，用虚拟语气）

到我们起床上学的时候了。

It is 10 years since he left home.（it表时间，since引导状语从句）

他自离开家以来有10年了。

It won't be long before he comes back from America.（it表时间，before引导状语从句）

不久以后他就从美国回来了。

It is very important for him to carry out proper amounts of exercise regularly.（it作形式主语）

对他来说，有规律地进行适度的锻炼是很重要的。

It was reported / said / thought / suggested / known / supposed / believed / that...（it作形式主语）

It is the first time that he has been to a foreign country.（it可用this，that代替，that引导定语从句，注意主句一般时、从句现在完成时）

这是他第一次去外国。

It was the first time that he had been to a foreign country.（it可用this，that代替，that引导定语从句，注意主句一般过去时、从句过去完成时）

这是他第一次去外国。

It was in a company where his father had worked that he was promoted.（it was...that为强调句型，where引导的定语从句）

他是在他父亲曾经工作过的公司被提拔的。

It was not until he came back home last night that we went to bed.（it was...that为强调句型，强调until时，把not一并提前）

昨晚直到他回来我们才上床睡觉。

二、倒装结构

有时候为了强调或者语法上的需要，把谓语或者谓语的一部分提到主语之前，这就是倒装结构。倒装分为完全倒装（complete inversion）和部分倒装（partial inversion）。

1. 完全倒装

（1）把谓语动词直接提到主语之前，称为完全倒装。最常见的完全倒装需要下列三个条件：

第一，句首要有表处所、方向等的副词或介词短语，如：up，down，in，out，here，there，in the sky，on the wall，out of the room，etc。

第二，所用动词是不带宾语的不及物动词，如：come，go，run，rush，fly，sit，lie，stand，etc。

第三，动词时态仅限一般现在时和一般过去时，其他时态一般不用。

Here comes the bus.

公共汽车来了。

There goes the bell.

铃响了。

Out rushed all the students after the bell rang.

铃响之后所有学生冲出教室。

There lies a beautiful small town at the foot of the mountain.

那山脚下有一座美丽的小城。

Out of the classroom ran the little boy student.

那个小男学生跑出了教室。

From the valley came a frighting sound.

从山谷里传来一个吓人的声音。

On the wall hang two large portraits.

墙上挂着两幅肖像。

（2）如果主语是代词，只把副词或介词短语放置句首，主谓语不倒装。例如：

Here he comes.

他来了。

Out she rushed，with a baby in her arms.

她冲了出来，怀里抱着一个婴儿。

（3）为了句子衔接或者更加合理，有时候把作表语的形容词、过去分词、不定式或介词短语置于句首，其后用完全倒装。

Present at the meeting were experts from all over the world.

出席会议的专家来自世界各地。

Gone are the days when they had no food to eat and no clothes to wear.

他们没吃没穿的日子一去不复返了。

Among the presents are watches，sunglasses and some toys.

那些礼物包括手表、太阳镜和玩具。

（4）其他完全倒装形式。

第一，There be / live / exist / stand / lie...等句型中，例如：

Once upon a time **there lived** a king who loved horses very much.

从前，那里生活着一位非常喜欢马的国王。

There existed a tall tree about 10 years ago，but later it was cut down for some reason.

大约10年前，那儿有一棵大树，后来因故被砍倒了。

第二，Such + be +主语结构中，动词be的人称与数和后面的主语保持一致，例如：

Such is the fact that nobody agreed with him at the meeting.

事实就是这样：会上没人同意他的意见。

Such are my students，a group of clever and lovely boys and girls.

我的学生就是这样：一群聪明可爱的孩子。

第三，直接引语后的短句子，主语是名词时完全倒装，主语是代词时不倒装，例如：

"I don't agree with what you have discussed," **declared** Mr. Johnson.

"我不同意你们讨论的东西。"约翰逊先生宣布说。

"As far as I know，English is not very difficult to learn," she said gently.

"据我所知，英语不太难学。"她轻声地说。

第四，在一些表示祝愿的句子中。例如：

Long live the Communist Party of China！

中国共产党万岁！

Long live the People's Republic of China!

中华人民共和国万岁!

2. 部分倒装

部分倒装就是把系动词、情态动词以及助动词提到主语之前。下列几种情况需要部分倒装:

(1) only放置句首强调除主语以外的其他成分时,需要部分倒装,因为only后可以是短语,也可以是从句。如果是从句,倒装后面的主句。例如:

Only in this way can we learn English well.

只有通过这种方式我们才能学好英语。

Only then did I understand what he had meant.

只有到那个时候我才理解他的用意。

Only when she had her own child **did she realize** how painful and hard her parents had been.

只有当她有了自己的孩子,她才意识到她的父母是多么的辛苦。

Only doctors can save your life and make you recover yourself. (only强调主语时不倒装)

只有大夫才能救你的命并且使你恢复健康。

(2) 用so,neither,nor引起部分倒装。

第一,当表示前一个人或物的情况同样适合于后一个人或物时,两个句子中的时态、助动词、情态动词要一致;肯定句中用so,否定句中用neither或nor。例如:

My father is a doctor. **So is** my mother.

我爸爸是大夫。妈妈也是。

If you don't go to the movies tonight, **neither** shall I.

如果你今晚不去看电影,我也不去。

第二,如果原句中既有否定又有肯定,或者既有实义动词又有系动词等情况的时候,用so it is (the same) with 或so it was (the same) with结构。例如:

He is a middle school teacher but he doesn't like teaching. **So it is with** his brother.

他是中学教师,但他不喜欢教书。他哥哥也是如此。

She went to America five years ago and she hasn't been heard of ever since. **So it was with** him.

她五年前去了美国，从此再没有收到她的消息。他也是一样。

第三，如果是为了加强语气，句子不用倒装，只把so放置句首就行。例如：

—Look! The young man is as strong as a cattle.

瞧！那位年轻人壮如牛啊。

—So he is.

确实是。

—The girl standing there looks beautiful and elegant.

站在那边的女孩看上去既漂亮又优雅。

—So she does and so do you.（前一句加强语气，后一句倒装）

她真的是啊，你也一样。

（3）否定意义的副词和介词短语置于句首时要部分倒装，常见的副词有：little, never, not, seldom, no longer, nowhere, hardly, barely, scarcely, no sooner, not only, in no way, in no case, on no account, etc。例如：

Little did he care about his own safety, though the teacher was in danger himself.

尽管老师自己也处于危险之中，但他对自己的安危一点都不在乎。

Never once have the couple quarreled with each other in their 40-year marriage life.

这老两口在40年的婚姻生活中从没吵过一次架。

Not a single mistake should we make in our composition.

我们在作文中一个错都不应该犯。

Not until midnight did he come back from his office.

直到午夜他才从办公室回来。

Not until he came back home did we go to bed.（因until后可以是短语也可以是从句，是从句时倒装后面的主句）

直到他回家我们才去睡觉。

Seldom does he come to school late, but he did today.

他上学很少迟到，但今天迟到了。

No longer will he stay in the People's Republic of China.

他将不再待在中华人民共和国了。

Nowhere can you find the toy that I have bought for your birthday.

你在任何地方都找不到我给你买的生日礼物玩具。

Hardly/Barely/Scarcely had he finished his homework when the bell rang.

他刚做完作业，铃就响了。

No sooner had she arrived home than a terrible rainstorm came.

她刚到家里，一场可怕的暴风雨来了。

Not only were the students interested in the game，but also their teacher was fond of it.

不仅学生们对这个游戏感兴趣，而且他们的老师也喜欢它。

In no way shall we give up hope，instead we should continue to work hard.

我们决不能放弃希望，相反我们要继续努力工作。

In no case should we turn against our homeland.

任何情况下我们都不应该背叛祖国。

On no account should we give in to difficulties in life and work.

我们决不应该屈服于生活和工作中的困难。

（4）在so/such...that...句型中，把so/such以及所修饰的词和短语提到句首，so，such所在句子的谓语要部分倒装。例如：

So fast does he run that nobody can catch up with him.

他跑得如此之快，以至于没有人能赶上他。

Such a lovely girl is she that many people like her.

她是如此可爱的一位女孩，以至于很多人都喜欢她。

So shallow a lake is it that no fish can survive in it.

这是如此浅的一个湖，以至于鱼无法在里面生存。

（5）as/though引导让步状语从句时，通常把从句中的一个词以及与之关系紧密的修饰语提到as / though之前，如果是单数可数名词，把名词提到句首，冠词省略。例如：

Hard as / though he tried，he didn't succeed eventually.

尽管他努力了，但他最终没有成功。

Perfectly well **as / though** he behaved in the competition，he didn't get any prize.

尽管他在比赛中表现得非常好，但他还是没能获奖。

Child as / though she is，she knows a lot about life.

尽管她是个孩子，但她了解很多关于生活的东西。

（6）在含有if的虚拟语气条件句中，如果从句中有were，had，should，可以省略if，把were，had，should提到句首。例如：

Were I you（If I were you），I would stay at home and watch TV every day.

我要是你的话，我会每天待在家里看电视。

Had he passed（If he had passed）the exam，he would have got the chance to study abroad.

他要是通过考试的话，就会得到出国学习的机会。

Should it rain（If it should rain），the crops would be saved.

天要是下雨的话，庄稼就会得救。

（7）在表示"越……越……"的句型中，把定冠词和形容词比较级放置句首，但主谓不倒装。例如：

The more we get together，**the happier** we will be.

我们聚得越多，我们就越高兴。

The longer we stay here，**the more** we like to stay here.

我们在这里待得越长就越想待在这里。

The larger vocabulary you have，**the easier** you will find it to enlarge it.

你会发现你词汇量越大，你就越容易扩大它。

（8）有些表祝愿的句子用倒装。例如：

May you succeed！

祝你成功！

三、省略

省略是一种普遍的语言现象，尤其在对话中，它有助于语言的简洁紧凑，避免重复。常见用法如下：

（1）if引导的虚拟语气从句中含有were，had，should时，省略if，把were，had，should提到句首，或者直接省略主句。例如：

Were I ten years younger, I would go to work there.

我要是年轻十岁的话，我会去那儿工作。

Had I met you yesterday, I would have told you the news.

我要是昨天遇见你的话，我会告诉你那个消息的。

Should he come back to himself, all his relatives and friends would be very happy.

他要是能醒过来，他所有的亲戚和朋友都会很开心。

If only he had a large house!

他要是有一栋大房子就好了！

If only he had passed the driving test!

他要是通过考试就好了！

（2）在交际用语中，通常省略重复部分或其他成分。例如：

—Mary is not coming to the party tonight.

玛丽今晚不来参加晚会了。

—But she promised.（to come to the party tonight）

但是她答应了呀。

—When did you meet with my father?

你什么时候遇见我父亲了？

—（I met with your father）Last Monday.

上周一。

—What about going out for a walk in the garden?

咱们出去到花园散步怎么样？

—（That's a）Good idea.

好主意。

—How long have you been in China?

你在中国待多久了？

—（I have been in China for）Five years.

五年了。

（3）有时候为了避免重复，常省略动词不定式中的动词及后面的部分。如果后面是一般动词保留到to，如果是动词不定式的完成式保留到to have，如果是系动词保留到to be。常见的有下列几种情况：

第一，在be + pleased，glad，anxious，eager，happy，willing，ready等形容词之后省略to之后的成分。例如：

—I will **be away** on a business trip. Would you mind looking after my cat?

我要出差，你介意照顾一下我的猫吗？

—Not at all. I'd **be happy** to.（look after your cat）

一点都不。我很乐意。

—Will you join us in the discussion?

你愿意和我们一起讨论吗？

—Yes. I'll **be glad** to.（join you in the discussion）

好，我很愿意。

第二，在动词tell/ask/persuade/permit/wish/advise/allow/order somebody to do something等跟动词不定式作宾语补足语的句子中省略to后面的成分。例如：

The little boy wanted to ride his bike in the street，but his mother **told** him not **to**.（ride his bike in the street）

那个小男孩想在街上骑自行车，但他妈妈告诉他不要去。

At first he didn't want to give up smoking，but finally he was **persuaded to**.（give up smoking）

起初他不想戒烟，但最终还是被说服了。

The teacher advised us to do what we are **allowed to**.（do）

那位老师建议我们做允许被做的事。

第三，在have to，need，ought to，be able to，be going to，used to中省略to之后的成分。例如：

We should do everything that we **ought to**.（do）

我们应该做我们该做的一切。

They didn't want to give up smoking but they **had to**.（give it up）

他们不想戒烟，但他们不得不。

—You **ought to** have finished your work by six yesterday.

你应该在昨天六点以前做完工作。

—Yes. I **ought to** have.（finished my work by six yesterday）

是的，我应该如此。

—Are you interested in TV plays?

你对电视剧感兴趣吗？

—No. But I **used to be**.（interested in TV plays）

不，但是我以前是。

第四，在动词love，like，mean，expect，want，wish，intend等后接动词不定式作宾语时省略to之后的成分。例如：

—You should have asked for a leave in person.

—你应该亲自请个假。

—I **meant** to（ask for a leave in person），but when I was leaving I couldn't find him anywhere.

我打算要请假，但我离开的时候，在任何地方找不到他。

Although my parents don't **expect** me to become a doctor，but I want to.（become a doctor）

尽管我父母不希望我成为一名医生，但我想。

（4）在感官动词see，watch，hear，feel，notice，observe，listen to，look at以及使役动词have，make，let后接动词不定式作宾语补足语时省略to。例如：

I saw some boys and girls **enter** the classroom.

我看见一些孩子进了教室。

The boss makes his employees **work** more than ten hours a day.

那位老板使他的员工每天工作十个小时以上。

（5）当主句和从句的主语一致或者从句中是it is / was时，经常用状语从句的省略形式，即"连词+形容词、现在分词、过去分词"等，常用连词有：when，whenever，while，as，once，if，unless，though，although，even if，even though，as if，as though，where，wherever，etc。与主句主语之间是主动关系时用现在分词，是被动关系时用过去分词。例如：

While crossing the street，you'd better look to the left and then to the right.

当你过马路时，最好先向左看，再向右看。

When asked how old she was，she just kept silent.

当有人问她几岁时，她只是保持沉默。

Once staged，the play will prove another great success.

这个剧一旦被搬上舞台，将会证明又是一个巨大的成功。

Don't speak until spoken to.

不要说话，直到有人对你说话。

Though invited formally，she didn't come to the dinner party the other day.

尽管被正式邀请了，但她那天还是没有来参加宴会。

She cried sadly as if emotionally hurt by her boyfriend.

她伤心地哭着，仿佛被男朋友在情感方面伤了。

Fill the blanks with articles where necessary.

必要的地方填上冠词。

（6）在主从复合句中，引导宾语从句的that常常省略；引导定语从句的关系代词whom，that，which作宾语时常常省略；引导定语从句的关系副词that也常常省略。例如：

I believe（that）Mr. Johnson will come to help us this afternoon.

我相信约翰逊先生下午将来帮我们。

This is the company（which / that）we visited last October.

这是去年十月我们参观过的那家公司。

There was no one in the street（whom）she could turn to for help.

街上没有她可以求助的人。

I don't like the way（that）you treat elderly people.（that是关系副词，表方式）

我不喜欢你对待老年人的方式。

This is the first time（that）I have attended such a lecture.（that是关系副词，表时间）

这是我第一次参加这样的报告。

It is high time（that）we took a good rest.（that是关系副词，表时间）

到了该我们好好休息一下的时候了。

（7）在表示"建议、主张、命令、要求"等意义的动词有关的名词性从句中，用should+动词原形表示虚拟语气，should可以省略。例如：

It's required in the regulations that all the students（**should**）not carry mobile phones at school.

规定要求所有学生上学期间不得带手机。

He insisted that the students（**should**）read English aloud every morning.

他主张学生们应该每天早晨大声朗读英语。

His request is that all the teachers（**should**）offer their good ideas about teaching.

他请求所有的老师把自己关于教育的好点子奉献出来。

He put forward the suggestion that we（**should**）give up smoking and drinking.

他提出了我们应该戒烟戒酒的建议。

（8）感叹句中有时候可以省略主语和谓语。例如：

What a hot day（it is）!

多热的天啊！

How beautiful（they are）!

多漂亮啊！

（9）为了使句子更加清晰明了，并列句中常常省略与前一句中相同的部分。例如：

One of the sides of the board should be painted yellow, and the other（of the sides should be painted）white.

这块板子的一面应该漆成黄色，另一面漆成白色。

Some people like to work in the morning, but others（like to work）in the afternoon.

一些人喜欢上午工作，而另一些人喜欢下午（工作）。

（10）在对话中，动词和短语think, expect, believe, suppose, guess, imagine, hope, be afraid, fear等后用so代替一个词、短语或句子，用not可以代替一个否定意义的句子。例如：

—Look at the dark clouds in the sky. It is going to rain soon.

瞧天上的乌云，马上要下雨了。

—I **hope** so.

我希望如此。

—The boy has been preparing for the interview for a long time and he's sure to succeed.

这个男孩为面试准备了好长时间，他肯定能成功。

—I **believe** so.

我相信会的。

—You haven't lost the ticket for the movie, have you?

你不会把电影票丢了吧?

—I **hope** not. It's difficult to get another one at the moment.

我希望没有，这会儿再买一张不容易啊。

但think, expect, believe, suppose, imagine的否定式有两种，即I think not. 和 I don't think so.而 guess, hope, be afraid, fear的否定式只有一种，即I hope not.

（11）其他省略形式有：What for? So what? What if? Why not? How come? Pardon? if so, if not, if ever, if any, etc。例如：

—I have to go back to the classroom.

我不得不回一趟教室。

—**What for**?

为什么?

—You missed the lecture given by Mr. White.

你错过了怀特先生的报告。

—**So what**? It's very boring.

那又怎么样? 很乏味的。

What if he doesn't agree to the plan?

倘若他不同意计划怎么办?

—Let's go to the cinema to relax ourselves tonight.

咱们今晚去看电影，轻松一下。

—**Why not**?

好啊!

—He fell off the bicycle in the street yesterday.

他昨天在街上从自行车上摔下来了。

—**How come**?

怎么回事?

—The train will remain at this station from two o'clock.

火车从两点起停在这个车站。

—**Pardon**? I didn't follow you.

你再说一下,我没听懂。

—The weather forecast says it will continue to rain for some days in the near future.

天气预报说近期内会一直下雨。

—**If so**,our crops will be damaged by the flood.

如果这样的话,我们的庄稼会被毁掉的。

—He is ill now and we wonder if he will recover soon.

他生病了,我们想知道他会不会马上康复。

—**If not**,we'd better appoint another one to take his place.

如果不康复的话,我们得派别人接替他。

—Can you lend me some money?

你能借给我一点钱吗?

—Sorry. **If any**,I certainly will.

很抱歉。如果有的话,我一定会的。

—Does she often come late for class?

她经常上课迟到吗?

—No. **If ever**,once a year at most.

没有,要是有的话,也就最多一年一次。

Why argue with her? She's a gossip.

你为什么跟她吵啊? 她是个长舌妇。

Why not go to bed early and get up early?

你为什么不早睡早起?

—Tom,go and clean the table.

汤姆,你去擦桌子。

—Why me? John is sitting there doing nothing at all.

为什么是我呀？约翰坐在那儿，一点事都没有。

=Why do you have me go and clean the table? John is sitting there doing nothing at all.

你为什么要我去收拾桌子？约翰坐在那儿，一点事都没有。

Exercise Sixteen

（一）单句语法填空

1. —Mr. Johnson asked me to remind you of the meeting this afternoon. Don't forget it!

   —OK. I_____.

2. When _____（compare）with other athletes, he has the perfect body shape for a swimmer.

3. —May I smoke here?

   —If you _____, choose a seat in the smoking section.

4. It was not until she got home _____ Jennifer realized she had lost her keys.

5. —I was wondering if we could go skiing on the weekend.

   —_____（sound）good.

6. No sooner had the teacher left the classroom _____ Tom broke the window.

7. It is widely believed that the sense of achievement of people has little, if _____, to do with the amount of money.

8. _____ he free tomorrow, he would help you with your work.

9. At the foot of the mountain _____（lie）a small village.

10. Why! I have nothing to confess（坦白）.What is it _____ you want me to say?

（二）单句改错

1. Look! Here come the bus.

2. Only when I graduated from the high school did I realized that I was wrong.

3. Hardly had I reached the bus stop than the bus started.

4. Little he care about what others think about him.

5. I saw the interesting and exciting film last week. So does she.

6. Not until Mr. Smith came to China didn't he know what kind of country China is.

7. Hero as he is a, he has some shortcomings.

8. When crossed the street, you'd better look to the left and then to the right.

9. Not only did everything he had taken away from him, but also his German citizenship.

10. Among them were a soldier who was wounded in the stomach.

（三）语法填空

阅读下面材料，在空白处填入适当的内容（1个单词）或括号内单词的正确形式。

Long ago, there was a mother and a son ___1___ （live） in a house. She worked hard every day, ___2___ they were always poor.

One day, her son stole his friend's bag. "Mom, what do you think of this bag？" His mother praised her son instead of scolding him. The next time, he stole an overcoat. She praised him again. A few years ___3___ （late）, he grew up to be a young man. He stole a piece of jewelry and brought it to his mother. This time, she ___4___ did not scold her son. Then, he started to steal more expensive things.

One day, the police caught him. Before he ___5___ （put） in prison, he begged the police to meet his mother. They took him to his mother. As soon as he saw his mother, he suddenly ___6___ （bite） her ear. "Ouch！ What is the matter with you？" She finally scolded him. Her son answered, "If you ___7___ （give） me a scolding like that when I stole the first bag, I could not have become a thief."

___8___ （look） at her son heading to prison, "If only I ___9___ turn back time, I would scold him severely," she said ___10___ （regret）.

（四）短文改错

Dear Mr. Xie,

I'm very exciting to write to you to express my thanks. I am Li Hua, one of the poor children who was crying for knowledge, but couldn't afford the school fees because my father was ill or my family was deeply in debt. Thank you for give me generous support so that I could have the chance go back to school. Has it not been for the support, I wouldn't have realized my dream. Your help makes much difference to me. I am sure to spread the love to help people in the need.

In brief, my appreciation for your kindness can never be expressed in word. Please accept my sincerely gratitude.

Yours,

Li Hua

第十七章　There be结构&It的用法

一、There be结构

（1）There be结构表示"某处存在某物"，there没有实际意义，属于倒装句，谓语是be动词，后面的名词通常用就近一致原则；be可以根据需要变成各种时态，也可以被其他词替换，如：seem to be，happen to be，exist，sit，stand，live，lie，remain，enter，follow，etc。例如：

There is a pencil-box，two picture books and three dictionaries on the desk.（就近一致）

桌子上有一个铅笔盒、两本图画书和三本字典。

There will be a very interesting film tonight.

今晚将有一部很有趣的电影。

There has been an old temple on that high mountain.

一直以来，那座高山上都有一座旧庙。

There seems to be something wrong with my computer，doesn't there？

我的电脑好像有点毛病，是吗？

There stands a high building which was built many years ago.

那里矗立着很多年前建成的一栋高楼。

There lie two dragons named the Yangtze River and the Yellow River.

那里盘着的两条龙是长江与黄河。

There lived a king who liked paintings very much a long time ago，didn't there？

很久以前那儿生活着一位非常喜欢画的国王，是吗？

There followed a loud noise，which made people very frightened.

使人们很害怕的一声巨响随之而来。

There being no bus or taxi in the street，I had to walk home. （逗号不能连接两个简单句，故用独立主格结构）

因为街上没有公共汽车和出租车了，我不得不走回家。

I have never dreamed of **there being** a flower on my desk.（介词后用动名词复合结构）

我做梦也没想到我桌子上有一朵花。

（2）其他含有there be的常见句型。例如：

There is no point in arguing with them further.

跟他们继续争论下去没有意义。

There is no doubt that you will be admitted to a key university if you work hard.

毫无疑问，只要努力学习，你将会被重点大学录取。

There is no use in trying to persuade him to give up smoking.

企图说服他戒烟是没有用的。

There is no need to worry about your future.

你没必要为自己的未来担忧。

There is no sense in making her apologize to us.

强迫她向我们道歉是没有道理的。

二、It的用法

it的用法一直是考点之一，也是英语中出现频率很高的一个词，下面就将it的最常见用法列举如下。

1. it用作人称代词

it指前文提到的单数物体、不可数名词、事情、this、that以及性别不明的小孩、做某个动作的人，一般属于特指。例如：

He bought **a new apartment** and it needs to be decorated and furnished.

他买了一套楼房，房子需要装修和布置摆设。

She offered me **some bread** but I couldn't accept it.

她主动给我面包，但我不能接受它。

He told us he had **been** seriously **criticized** by the teacher and **it** surprised us very much.

他告诉我们他被老师严肃批评，这件事使我们很震惊。

—What's this / that?

这（那）是什么？

—It's a compass.

这（那）是指南针。

It is just a one-month-old baby. Don't shout at **it**.

他只是个刚满月的婴儿。不要大声冲着他叫嚷。

—Who is making such a noise?

谁在大声吵闹？

—It must be the children.

一定是那些孩子。

2. it用作非人称代词

it指时间、天气、气候、温度、地点、距离等。例如：

It was ten o'clock p.m. when we arrived at the hotel last night.

昨晚我们到旅馆的时候已经十点钟了。

It is fine today and tomorrow. You can go out for a tour.

今明两天天晴，你可以出去走走看看。

It is not cold in winter and not very hot in summer here.

这儿冬天不冷，夏天不热。

It has been up to 35 degrees centigrade on average here for more than ten days.

十天多来，这儿的温度一直平均高达35摄氏度。

It is the Lanzhou Railway Station built about 30 years ago.

这就是大约30年前建成的兰州火车站。

It is 20 miles from here to the railway station.

从这儿到火车站有20英里的距离。

3. it用作先行代词——作形式主语

（1）作形式主语时，it代替后面由主语从句、动词不定式、动名词充当的真正主语，使句子显得流畅平衡。例如：

It is a pity that you didn't come to attend the lecture given by Professor White.

你没来听怀特教授做的报告是件遗憾的事情。

It is very necessary and important for us to do regular exercise every day.

对我们来说，每天进行有规律的锻炼是必要而且重要的。

It is very nice of you to help me with my English.

你帮我学英语，你真好。

It is no use crying over spilt milk.

覆水难收。

（2）常用动名词作真正主语的形容词和名词有：nice，good，useless，enjoyable，worthwhile以及use，good，fun，job，task，a waste of time，etc。例如：

It is **nice** talking to you and your family.

跟你及你的家人交谈真是愉快。

It is **fun** jumping into water to have a swim in such hot weather.

这么热的天，跳进水里游泳真爽。

It is **worthwhile** making a mistake if we can learn something from it.

如果能从错误中学点什么，这个错就犯得值。

（3）it作形式主语的其他常见句型。例如：

It is **likely / possible / probable** that a heavy rain is coming soon.

一场大雨可能马上就来。

It **looks as if** it is going to rain tonight.

看样子今晚仿佛要下雨。

It **appears / seems** that she had heard of the bad news.（用虚拟语气）

她好像已经听说这个坏消息了。

It **happened** that he had enough money on him at that moment.

那时碰巧他身上带了足够多的钱。

It **occurred to** me that I had left my handbag in the taxi.

我突然想起，我把手包落在出租车上了。

It is **no wonder** that she has passed such a difficult exam.

难怪她通过了如此难的考试。

It is **up to** her to decide who will be chosen as her assistant.

由她负责决定谁将被选为她的助手。

4. it用作先行代词——作形式宾语

（1）作形式宾语时，it代替后面由动词不定式、动名词以及宾语从句充当的真正宾语，使句子显得流畅平衡。例如：

I **think** it impossible for him to be chosen as manager of our company.

我认为他被选拔为我们公司经理的可能性不大。

Don't you consider it **wrong** wasting your time like that?

难道你不认为你那么浪费时间是错误的吗？

We have made it **a rule** that we mustn't watch TV while having meals.

我们把吃饭时不看电视定为一个规矩。

We take it **for granted** that all the people would like to help each other.

我们想当然地认为，所有的人都愿意相互帮助。

（2）it作形式宾语时，一般其后接有形容词或者名词充当的宾语补足语，然后接真正宾语，但下列动词和短语的形式宾语it后没有宾语补足语，直接跟从句，这类动词和短语有：like，love，enjoy，hate，dislike，appreciate，resent（憎恶），swallow（容忍），have（坚持说），put（提议），swear，let out，hide，see to，rely on，depend on，count on。例如：

I don't **like** it that she is not only careless but also impolite to seniors.

我不喜欢她不仅粗心而且对长辈不礼貌的特点。

I'd **appreciate** it if you can lend me more books to read.

如果你借给我更多的书来读的话，我会感谢你。

Shakespeare **had** it that all the world is a big stage.

莎士比亚说整个世界是个大舞台。

We will **see to** it that all the students go out of the teaching building safely.

我们要保证所有的学生安全地走出教学楼。

We **rely on** / **depend on** it that you will come and help us.

我们需要你的到来和帮助。

I'm **counting on** it that you will turn up soon.

我正期待你马上出现。

（3）it在"动词＋介词短语"构成的固定短语中作形式宾语，把宾语从句放置句末，常用短语有：leave it to...，owe it to...，bear it in mind，put it to...，rub it into...，put it into sb.'s head，etc。例如：

I **leave it to** his own judgement whether he should choose the position.

我让他自己判断他是否该选择那份工作。

I **owe it to** my parents that I have been successful in my career.

我把自己事业的成功归功于父母。

We should always **bear it in mind** that many accidents arise from drunk driving.

我们应该牢记，很多事故发生于酒驾。

He **put it to** all the students whether they should learn Module Nine.

他让所有学生考虑他们是否学习第九模块。

The teacher **rubbed it into** them that reading aloud was very important to language learning.

老师向他们一再强调朗读对语言学习非常重要。

Something **put it into** his head that she was not honest.

有件事使他突然想起她不诚实。

5. it用于强调句式中

It is Miss Mary that / who often helps us with our English.

是玛丽小姐经常帮我们学英语。

It was not until she took off her dark glasses that I could recognize her.

直到她摘下墨镜，我才认出她。

Was **it** in the classroom that he smoked yesterday?

他昨天是在教室吸烟的吗?

Where was **it** that you met with my father the other day?

你那天到底在哪里遇见我父亲的?

Can you tell me what **it** was that made you lose your interest in studies?

你能告诉我到底是什么使你失去学习兴趣的吗?

Exercise Seventeen

（一）单句语法填空

1. There _____（stand）a high mountain which is very beautiful.

2. _____ is no doubt that you will be admitted into Peking University if you work hard.

3. —Who is making so much noise in the garden?

—_____ is the children.

4. _____ is our belief that improvements in health care will lead to a stronger, more prosperous economy.

5. It was evening _____ we reached the little town of Winchester.

6. The chairman thought _____ necessary to invite Professor Smith to speak at the meeting.

7. The doctor advised Vera strongly that she should take a holiday, but _____ didn't help.

8. What a pity! My computer doesn't work. _____ must be something wrong with it.

9. I took _____ for granted that he would believe in us.

10. _____ is no need for us to discuss the problem since it has already been settled.

（二）单句改错

1. Nowadays, there have a lot of valuable books in the school library for us to borrow.

2. This is very important and necessary for us to read English aloud every day.

3. I'd appreciate if you would like to teach me how to use the computer.

4. That occurred to me that I had left my keys in the office.

5. What is a fact that English is being accepted as an international language.

6. They are three lessons in the morning and two in the afternoon in my dream school.

7. There are a dictionary, two books, three magazines and some newspapers.

8. I think that a good idea to get up early.

9. It is no use cry over spilt milk.

10. There was no bus or taxi in the street last night, I had to walk home.

（三）语法填空

阅读下面材料，在空白处填入适当的内容（1个单词）或括号内单词的正确形式。

Everyone knows that earthquakes can damage their property. But actually, in some situations, more damage is done after an earthquake than when it ____1____ (happen). However, you can do a great many things ____2____ an earthquake that may help to protect your home. Firstly, make sure ____3____ is no gas leak. The professional suggestion is to turn off the gas line if you can. If there is a gas leak and you can't turn it off, ____4____ is recommended that you get everyone out of the house ____5____ go to a neighbor's to call the fire department. Secondly, make sure none of the water pipes are broken. Even if you don't see any water leaking, you should call the water company to see ____6____ the water is safe to drink. You don't want any one of your family members to get sick because he or she has drunk ____7____ (safe) water, right? The last thing you should do is ____8____ (make) sure the foundation of the house is not cracked or sinking. A cracked or sinking foundation can be a sign ____9____ the house may collapse. In that case, leave the house and do not enter ____10____ until an expert looks at the problem.

（四）短文改错

Nowadays, the computer technology develops very fast that the Internet has become more and more popular. Some students regard them as a great helper. Because there has a lot of information on line, so you can surf the Internet for any information you need in a short time without working hard in the library. This is also very convenient to talk with others by using the Internet. However, other students think that there was some information on line which is not good for students. In addition, spend too much time playing games will not only have a bad effect on their studies but also do harm for health. Therefore, we should make properly use of the Internet. It is of great important to separate good plants from wild weeds.

第十八章　主谓一致

主谓一致是指谓语动词在人称和数方面与主语保持一致，它是贯穿英语学习整个过程的一种现象，也是中学英语语法学习中的难点，尤其在学生写作中体现得较多。主谓一致通常可以分为三种：形式一致、就近一致和意义一致。

一、形式一致

形式一致即主语是复数，谓语动词就用复数；主语是单数，谓语动词就用单数；主语是不可数名词，谓语动词也用单数。例如：

I **am** a middle school student and he **is** a university student.

我是一名中学生，他是一名大学生。

We all like playing football while **they are** fond of surfing the Internet.

我们都喜欢踢足球而他们喜欢上网。

A great many teachers **have been** praised by the local government.

很多教师已经被当地政府表彰。

A certain person **is asking** for you at the school gate.

学校门口有个人要见你。

Bread serves as main food in this area and tea **is** the main drink.

面包在这个地方是主食，茶是主要饮品。

二、就近一致

就近一致主要用在either...or...，neither...nor...，not only...but also...，not...but...连接两个主语以及there be 结构中，谓语与离得更近的一个主语保持一致。例如：

Either you or I **am** going to be sent to work in that rural area.

要么你，要么我，将被派到那个遥远的地方去工作。

Are either you or I going to be sent to work in that rural area？（谓语离you更近，故与之一致）

是我还是你将被派到那个遥远的地方工作呢？

Neither he nor his students **are** interested in the topic.

他和他的学生都对这个话题不感兴趣。

Not only his students but also he himself **was** praised by the president.

不仅他的学生而且他本人都被校长表扬了。

Not you but your wife **has been invited** to make a speech at the meeting.

不是你而是你妻子已经被邀请在会上发言。

There is a dictionary，two books，three pencil-boxes and some other things on the desk.

桌子上有一本字典、两本书、三个铅笔盒和别的一些东西。

There **stands** a tall tree and some old houses.

那儿矗立着一棵大树和一些旧房子。

三、意义一致

（1）表示时间、距离、价格、重量、温度等数目的名词作主语且表示整体概念时，谓语动词通常用单数。例如：

Two hours in exams is short while twenty minutes for waiting seems quite long.

考试中的两个小时很短而等待时的二十分钟却很长。

Fifty miles is a long way for us to walk.

五十英里路对我们步行来说是很长的一段路。

One hundred dollars for such a shirt is too expensive.

一百美元买这样一件衬衫有点太贵。

Fifty kilograms is too much for such a little girl to carry.

这么小的女孩扛五十千克有点太重了。

Forty degrees centigrade is the highest for the climate here.

四十摄氏度是这个地方的最高温度了。

（2）动词不定式、动名词以及主语从句作主语时，谓语动词用单数。例如：

When and where **to hold** the important meeting hasn't been decided yet.

什么时候、什么地点开这个要会还没有定下来。

Reading books is what I like most in my life.

读书是我一生最喜欢的事。

Why she has so many complains about the life **remains** to be seen.

她为什么对生活有那么多抱怨有待于验证。

（3）不定代词someone，anyone，no one，everyone，somebody，anybody，nobody，everybody，something，anything，nothing，everything作主语时，谓语动词用单数。例如：

Nothing is permitted while everything is allowed.

一切不准许，可是又被允许。

（4）every，each，no，many a修饰两个单数名词时，谓语动词用单数。例如：

Every boy and every girl is about to attend primary school according to the regulations.

根据规定，每个男孩女孩都应该上学。

No man and no woman has been admitted to the company this year.

今年这家公司男性女性都没招收。

Each father and **each** mother is going to attend the training meeting next week.

每位父亲和母亲下周都将参加培训会。

Many a teacher and **many** a student was invited to the party last night.

很多老师和学生昨晚被邀请到晚会上。

可以这样理解：Every boy and every girl = Every child；No man and no woman=No person；Each father and each mother = Each parent。所以谓语动词用单数。

（5）each，every，the whole，either，neither，more than one等跟单数名词连用或者each / either / neither + of + 复数名词时，谓语动词用单数。例如：

Each of us has an MP4 and every student likes listening to music on it.

我们每个人都有MP4，并且每个学生都喜欢听里面的音乐。

Either of my two sons is willing to be sent to work in Tibet.

我两个儿子中的任何一个都乐意被派到西藏去工作。

Neither of my parents has been chosen to attend the meeting.

父母中一个都没有被选上去参加会议。

More than one student has made that silly mistake.

不止一个学生犯了那个愚蠢的错误。

（6）and连接两个主语有时候谓语动词用单数。例如：

第一，and连接的两个名词表示必不可分的两部分时谓语动词用单数。例如：

All work **and** no play makes Jack a dull boy.

光工作不玩耍，聪明的孩子也会傻。

Bread **and** butter is what I need every day.

黄油面包是我每天都需要的东西。

A knife **and** fork is a western tool for meals.

一副刀叉是西方用餐工具。

A cart **and** horse was often seen in the past but not now.

马拉车在过去很常见，但现在没有了。

Needle **and** thread is always kept in her bag for use.

她的包里经常装有针线，以便随时使用。

第二，and连接的两个头衔之前共用一个冠词，表示一个人，谓语动词用单数。例如：

A poet **and** artist is coming to give us a lecture about painting today.

一位诗人兼艺术家今天要来给我们做关于油画的报告。

第三，and连接的两个头衔之前各用一个冠词，表示两个人，谓语动词用复数。例如：

The professor **and the** writer from Beijing University are going to give us lectures today.

北京大学的那位教授和那位作家今天都打算给我们做报告。

（7）主语后面如果有as well as, besides, rather than, but, except, along with, together with, in addition to, including, like, unlike等连用的短语时，谓

语动词仍然与前面的主语保持一致，也可以叫作"就远一致"。例如：

The teacher **as well as** the students likes the paintings.

老师和学生一样，也喜欢油画。

He **rather than** you was referred to at the meeting just now.

刚才会上提到的是他而不是你。

All **but** one in my office were invited to the dinner party yesterday.

除一人外，所有的人昨天都被邀请到宴会上了。

She **together with** her parents is going to pay a visit to Beijing next month.

她和父母下个月将一起去参观北京。

She **like** her elder sister doesn't like mathematics.

她和姐姐一样，不喜欢数学。

（8）关系代词在定语从句中作主语时，其谓语动词与先行词保持一致。

例如：

I，who am a teacher，**like** my pupils and teaching.

我是老师，我喜欢我的学生和教学工作。

You，who are a doctor，**like** your job and are patient with your patients.

你是医生，你喜欢你的工作，对病人有耐心。

She，who is a nurse，**is busy working** every day for the patients.

她是护士，每天为病人忙前忙后。

Please give the money to **those** who badly **need** it.

请把这钱给那些急需钱的人。

Please give the money to **anyone** who badly **needs** it.

请把这钱给任何急需钱的人。

He is **one of** the students who **are working** hard.（先行词是students）

他是努力学习的学生中的一位。

He is **the only one** of the students who has an expensive car.（先行词是the only one）

他是学生中唯一有一辆昂贵车子的人。

（9）集体名词作主语时，如果指集体或者整体概念，谓语动词用单数，指集体中的具体成员时，谓语动词用复数，常用的名词有：class，group， family, army, government, team, crew, company, committee, couple, audience, enemy, party, etc。例如：

The **family** is a big and excellent one in this neighbourhood.

这个家庭是该街区一个大而好的家庭。

The **family** are watching the live program on TV at the moment.

家庭成员们正在电视上看现场直播的节目。

The **government** has passed a lot of laws to protect the environment.

政府已经通过许多法律来保护环境。

The **government** are busy working every day to provide better service for the people.

政府官员们每天忙着工作，以便为人民提供更好的服务。

The **couple** has lived a happy life since they got married.

这对夫妻自结婚以来一直过着幸福的生活。

The **couple** were quarrelling with each other for a whole night last night.

这两口子昨天晚上一直在吵架。

但有些集体名词只能和复数动词连用，常见的有 people, police, cattle 等。例如：

The **police** are searching for the murderer.

警察正在搜找那个杀人犯。

People there don't have enough food to eat.

那儿的人没有足够的食物吃。

（10）定冠词加形容词表示一类人或物时，谓语动词用复数，但表单个人或物时，谓语动词用单数。例如：

The **old** are well taken care of in our country.

在我们国家老年人被照顾得很好。

The **dead** is his father-in-law.

死者是他岳父。

The **Chinese** are very intelligent, kind and hard-working.

中国人非常聪明、善良和勤劳。

The **Chinese** who has won Nobal Prize for literature is called Mo Yan.

获得诺贝尔文学奖的那位中国人叫莫言。

（11）分数和百分数以及 the rest, most / all / half + of + 名词时，谓语动词根据

名词而定，如果是可数名词，谓语动词用复数，如果是不可数名词谓语动词用单数。例如：

75% of the students in our class are girls.

我们班75%的学生是女孩子。

More than 70% of the surface of the earth is covered by water.

地球表面70%以上被水覆盖。

Four-fifths of the graduates have been employed in different units.

大学毕业生中的五分之四被不同单位录用。

Most of the teachers have been here，the rest are on the way here.

大部分老师已经到这儿了，其余的还在路上。

Half of the equipment has been transported there and the rest is going to be sent next week.

一半的设备已经被运往那里，其余的下周送过去。

四、其他主谓一致的情况

（1）the number of +复数名词的中心词是number，故谓语用单数；a number of +复数名词中的中心词是这个"复数名词"，故谓语动词用复数。例如：

The number of **the** books in the library **is** very large.（名词前要加定冠词之类的修饰语）

图书馆里书的数量很多。

A number of students **have gone to** the farm to help the farmers.（名词前没有其他修饰语）

许多学生已经去那个农场帮助农民了。

（2）a large quantity of +可数名词复数形式时谓语动词用复数，加不可数名词时谓语动词用单数；large / huge quantities of后无论加可数名词还是不可数名词，谓语动词都用复数；a large amount of +不可数名词，谓语动词用单数；large amounts of +不可数名词，谓语动词用复数。例如：

A large quantity of **books** have been distributed to those poor children.

大量的书已经分发给了那些贫穷的孩子。

A large quantity of land has been covered by sand.

大量的土地已经被沙子覆盖。

Large quantities of old magazines have piled up beside the desk.

大量的旧杂志已经堆在了桌子旁边。

Large quantities of food have been sent to the people in flood-stricken areas.

大量的食物已经被送给了遭洪水灾区的人们。

A large amount of money has been raised for those people.

大量的钱已经为那些人募捐起来了。

Large amounts of money have been given to them by the local government.

当地政府已经把大量的钱给了他们。

（3）what one needs...以及such...的谓语动词与后面的成分保持一致。例如：

What we need is a large sum of money.

我们所需要的是大笔的钱。

What we need are a great many books.

我们所需要的是很多书籍。

Such is the man，who is honest and hard-working.

这个人就是这样，诚实并且勤劳。

Such are the women，who wander from shop to shop buying nothing at all.

这些女人就是这样，从一个店逛到另一个店，什么都不买。

（4）means，works，sheep，fish，deer单复数相同，要根据句意选用动词。例如：

All possible means have been tried but every means is ineffective.

所有办法都试过了，但每个办法都没效率。

These fish are rare，so every fish is under protection.

这些鱼是罕见的，因此每条鱼都在保护之中。

（5）one and a half跟复数名词，但谓语动词用单数；a pair of后跟复数名词，谓语动词也用单数。例如：

One and a half days is all I can spare.

我能抽出的仅有一天半时间。

A pair of trousers / shoes / gloves / glasses / compasses has cost me a lot of money.

一条裤子（一双鞋、一副手套、一副眼镜、一个圆规）花去我好多钱。

（6）population表示整体时，谓语动词用单数，但population表示其中一部分时，谓语动词用复数。例如：

What's the population of China?

中国人口是多少？

The population of China is very large while the population of Japan is quite small.

中国人口很多而日本人口却相当少。

（7）all指人时谓语动词用复数，指物时用单数。例如：

Since all are here, let's begin our business.

既然大家都在这儿，那咱们开始吧。

All is going on well in our new company.

我们新公司里的一切都进展顺利。

（8）kind，form，type，sort，species of +名词时，谓语动词取决于这些词的单复数，而不是后面的名词。例如：

The kind of books is popular with young people.

这种书受年轻人喜欢。

Some new forms of art have caused a heated discussion.

一些新的艺术形式已经引起了热烈的讨论。

（9）定冠词加姓氏复数，表示夫妇或者一家人，谓语动词用复数。例如：

The Smiths try to find as much time as possible to play with their children.

史密斯夫妇尽量找出更多时间跟孩子们一起玩。

The Johnsons love music and all of them have attended different concerts.

杰克逊一家都喜欢音乐，并且都参加过不同的音乐会。

（10）表书名、地名等的复数名词谓语动词用单数。例如：

The United Nations is a useful organization to deal with some international issues.

联合国是一个处理国际问题的有用的组织。

Exercise Eighteen

（一）单句语法填空

1. The father as well as his three children _____ （go） skating on the frozen river every Sunday afternoon in winter.

2. Either you or the headmaster _____ （be） to hand out the prizes to these gifted students at the meeting.

3. Every possible means _____ （use） to prevent air pollution already, but the sky is still not clear.

4. 75% of the students _____ （have） been employed by different companies.

5. He is one of the boys who _____ （have） come here on time, but he is the only one who _____ （have） come with a notebook.

6. Many a professor and many a student _____ （be） looking forward to visiting China now.

7. Not the teacher but the students _____ （be） excited and happy.

8. Large quantities of money _____ （have） been given to the poor areas.

9. A large quantity of land _____ （have） been covered with snow.

10. A pair of glasses _____ （have） cost me 300 yuan.

（二）单句改错

1. Many a student have been praised by the headmaster.

2. Not only I but also Tom and Mary is fond of watching television.

3. When and where to build the new factory have not been decided yet.

4. Two fifths of the land in that district are covered with trees and grass.

5. The number of people invited were fifty, but a number of them were absent for different reasons.

6. Each man and each woman were asked to help when the fire broke out.

7. The injured in the tsunami is tourists from different parts of the world.

8. Climbing hills are of great help to people's health.

9. The United Nations are an important organization to deal with some serious problems throughout the world.

10. All means has been tried but every means is useless.

（三）语法填空

阅读下面材料，在空白处填入适当的内容（1个单词）或括号内单词的正确形式。

Our school library, along with many other buildings, is very different from other schools. There ___1___ （be） two computer rooms, three art rooms, a meeting room and a reading room in the library building. The number of the books ___2___ （be） large. It was 2, 000, 000 dollars ___3___ all the books cost our school. It is such a large amount of money ___4___ an average family can't afford it, right? But in my view, it is worth it because in the era of knowledge explosion, many students have a thirst for knowledge.

Our library is also a multifunctional building. There are 500 computers in it. Many a student ___5___ （surf） the Internet at weekends here and now you can see that my classmates, Mike and John, are surfing the Internet. ___6___ happy they are!

Look! A professor and writer ___7___ （be） delivering a speech in the meeting room. Every time there is a wonderful speech, the audience always ___8___ （cheer） up. What lovely children they are! Enter our art room and you will find a teacher with his students ___9___ （be） painting in the room. On the wall ___10___ （be） about 500 pictures, which attract many students.

（四）短文改错

Dear Frank,

I'm writing to tell you anything about my university life. It is three months since I come here. I have never left my parents for so long, but I miss them very much. At first it was difficult to me to do everything on my own, but now I am used to the life here. As for study, I major in the English because English is my favorite subject. I have made much good friends, one of whom are Jim, the most intelligent student in my class. He always has some good opinion and he is thought high of by others. I am sorry but I must to stop now. Please write to me when you are free.

Yours,

Li Hua